Thunder Through My Veins

GREGORY SCOFIELD

Thunder Through My Veins

MEMORIES OF A MÉTIS CHILDHOOD

A Phyllis Bruce Book
Harper*Flamingo*Canada

Quotations from poems are reproduced courtesy of
Polestar Book Publishers.

Cree words and phrases used in this book have been spelled
in their anglicized form.

http://www.harpercanada.com

HarperCollins books may be purchased for educational, business, or sales
promotional use. For information please write: Special Markets Department,
HarperCollins Canada, 55 Avenue Road, Suite 2900, Toronto,
Ontario, Canada M5R 3L2.

First HarperCollins hardcover ed. ISBN 0-00-200025-3
First HarperCollins trade paper ed. ISBN 0-00-638543-5

Canadian Cataloguing in Publication Data

Scofield, Gregory A., 1966–
Thunder through my veins: memories of a Métis childhood

"A Phyllis Bruce book".
ISBN 0-00-200025-3

1. Scofield, Gregory A., 1966– — Childhood and youth.
2. Poets, Canadian (English) — 20th century — Biography.*
3. Métis — Biography.
I. Title.

PS8587.C614Z53 1999   C811.54   C99-931141-7
PR9199.3.S297Z53 1999

99 00 01 02 03 04 HC 8 7 6 5 4 3 2 1

Printed and bound in the United States

For Mom Maria, whose courage, guidance, support, and love enabled me to dream; and for Patrick, my soul-father, who taught me to use the tools.

Between Sides

Where do I belong, way up north?
The first white trader
Must have felt this way

    on the reserve   a curio being looked over
    my skin defies either race   I am neither Scottish
    or Cree

So why those disgusted stares?
I speak the language
Eat my bannock with lard

    I am not without history   Half breed labour built
    this country   defending my blood has become a
    life-long occupation

White people have their own ideas
How a real Indian should look
In the city or on the screen

    I've already worked past that   came back to the
    circle   my way is not the Indian way or white way

I move in-between
Careful not to shame either side

—— *The Gathering: Stones for the Medicine Wheel*

Thunder Through My Veins

Foreword

The houses, hotels, shacks, and apartments where I grew up are too numerous to count though many of them loom in my memory like misshapen rocks, jagged with the indecipherable ghosts of my childhood which to this day remain so much a part of me. Others have faded over time, submerged in that river of my blood that has always been home.

The homes I most remember are the ones where my mother scattered her crocheted doilies and rag rugs, painted the rooms with the sorrowful lyrics of Kitty Wells, Hank Williams, and Wilf Carter, hung my grandmother's homemade curtains, pictures of the Yukon, sepia-coloured photos of her childhood, and various snapshots of our nomadic tribe captured like prisoners and staring their contempt from behind dust-covered frames. And always, wherever we were, Rembrandt's *Man with Golden Helmet* whom Mom called the "Iron Soldier," whose strong shadowed features and downcast eyes seemed to watch our every move, his golden helmet shining victoriously, a beacon of irony that I am sure spoke to her at the Salvation Army thrift store.

But there are also places and memories that belong to someone else — someone who looks identical to me — someone who survived the blackness that now seems so long ago. It is he, the boy I carry within, who remembers the years of separation, silence, and fear, the premature aging of my mother's face, the many towns where we sought refuge, the numerous homes where social workers, threats, and crashing fists followed us like a curse, a world where dreams of peace and safety lay shattered like the dishes on the kitchen floor. It is that world I've spent a lifetime running from, and that world I have finally begun to understand and accept.

Maple Ridge, the town where I was born and the place I have come back to, has, like me, changed and grown up. The hotels and apartments down by the river have vanished, giving way to the newer-looking condos and office buildings. Aunty Georgina's little shack has been transformed into an opulent castle — my memories of hot tea and bannock, songs and stories no longer there. The broken-down jalopies that were once the cadillacs of welfare kids have been hauled away as if they never existed. The dense thickets of willow, dogwood, and maple along River Road have been levelled and turned into subdivisions where families with money now live. Even the Fraser River has changed: its once treacherous waters now placid and resigned, laden with log booms that never seem to find their rightful place. Only the funeral chapel and the Chinese grocery up the street remain the same, enduring triumphantly like a few of the old-timers who have preserved themselves with the bootlegger's brew.

Walking now among the new and old, I sometimes see myself in the faces of today's children — children who despite their parents' wealth carry within them a different kind of poverty; they are survivors who, too, may one day write about their lives.

I have returned to Maple Ridge, my hometown, for one reason: I hope to find the little boy I left long ago. I hope to find his mother, tiny and frail, broken like the frame of the Iron Soldier, who despite her frailty led them from one war to the next. I hope to find peace with them, to finally give them words to speak their pain which until now has been a stone in my throat.

This is my story of survival and acceptance, of myself and my widening family. I write it for all of you who have survived and for those of you struggling to survive. Had it not been for the books I read as a teenager, I am sure I would not be at this place, today. Those very writers, people like Margaret Laurence, Maria Campbell, and Beatrice Culleton, made me want to write. They brought my mind and spirit to life. They gave me a sense of something larger than myself, something more profound than the pain, fear, and anger. They led me to a place of belonging, a permanent home where I have found a voice to speak with.

I have been writing and publishing books for seven years now. I am not very old and consider myself fortunate to have found my life's purpose, to see my dreams come true. The sacred ways of my great-grandmothers are just as much a part of my life as is the act of writing, and the healing I derive from it. In Cree, the story I am about to tell would be called *achee-mow-win*, which loosely translates to the telling of an everyday story, experience, or happening. Our creation stories, much like those of ancient tribal people, even the Bible itself, are known as *ah-tay-yow-kun*. They tell of the sacredness and power of the spirit world, of those very things which we as humans have little understanding and knowledge.

Ne-achee-moon (my story), like all stories, songs, dances, or any acts of creation, comes from the Thunderers, the Spirit-keepers of the West. Through dreams and visions I have been given guidance by them, and it is perhaps for this reason that I was chosen to be a writer, a storyteller. But, still young, I have much to learn, not only about storytelling but about life: its sacredness, its intricacies and mysteries, its beauty and ugliness.

In writing this book, I have encountered many difficult obstacles, most of which resulted from reliving the painful moments of my childhood. In some cases, notably my mother's early life, I have had to rely upon stories and recollections of family and those who knew her. Reconstructing her life before my birth has been much like putting together an incomplete puzzle, most of the pieces having gone to the grave with her.

However, the details and events in this book are as accurate as my memory can recall. For privacy reasons I have changed the names of those involved and occasionally details of their lives, all except for my great-great-grandparents, great-grandparents, grandparents, their siblings, my mother, and Aunty Georgina. Names of towns and institutions are accurate, as are the time sequences of my life. In this, I hope to bring you, the reader, into a world I often found disjointed and traumatic.

The river is good today, calm and peaceful. I stand before it, a mixture of blood and history running through my veins. I am neither from one nation nor the other, but from a nation that has struggled to define itself in the pages of Canadian history, in the face of continued denial and racism. In keeping the spirits of our great-great grandmothers alive, the first country wives of this land, we claim our aboriginal heritage and inherent rites, which have yet to be fully recognized by our Native and non-Native relations. In keeping with the hopes and dreams of our great-great-grandfathers, who fled to this land in search of political and religious freedom, prosperity, and new beginnings, we claim our rightful place as distinct yet valid people.

I am neither victim nor oppressor. The choices I have made in my adult life are mine alone. I blame only myself for the shame, anger, pity, and success that I have allowed. I speak for no one community, although my heartland, my ancestral and spiritual homeland, is among the scrub poplar and wolf willow rustling along the banks of the South Saskatchewan River, the fiddle as it echoes through the empty coulees at Batoche — the very place where my ancestors fought to keep our nation alive. I claim nothing except my place in the world, a place granted to me by the Thunderers, by the Celtic gods of a country I've never seen — those ancient spirits that live in the cells of my being.

The river is good today. Below the surface are the memories of a thousand years. Somewhere beneath its murky water lie the beginnings of my story and the words to tell it. It does not frighten me as it once did. I own each rock, each twig, each leaf, every bone that has collected on the bottom. The Thunderers of my great-great-grandmothers flourish in my veins, rumble from somewhere deep within — only this time, the spirit-keepers are with me.

One

Goodbye Before I've Begun

Everyone is sitting down for dinner; presents given.
A clown's tie comes to mind, maybe some tools for
The garage? A wrench seems so hard, unfeeling.

The mountains divide us neatly,
As good an excuse as any.
Having been to Winnipeg once, I thought about
The lost years. There are lots of Cree & Saulteaux
Filling up the city — mostly
Vacant-eyed kids.

Counting the scarring years, the jagged father-figures:
I could have easily become an island, stayed hidden.
Saying I should forget every fist, each hateful
Mouthful is to say I deserved it all. Even now, this
Day takes work: catch myself wondering how it might
Have been different if he'd stuck around.

My father's story is like the twisted roots of an old tree: roots that have crept into my own story, reaching those far-removed places within me that have forever kept him silent and dead. Even now, he is the voiceless crow who sits in the tree of his and my mother's making: a tree made whole by my mother's love and nurturing, a tree that has prospered without him.

His life was a mystery. No one, including Mom, knew much about him, his childhood and parents, even if he had siblings. He was said to be from Winnipeg and was reputed to be a big-time con man, well known in criminal circles. Mom claimed that he was connected with the underground world, dealing in counterfeit money, drugs, and stolen goods, that he pulled scams on everyone from the local barber to business executives. He had numerous alias names and warrants out for his arrest all across Canada and the U.S. The few glimpses she allowed of him stirred my imagination, and as a child I remember thinking of him as a shadowy character in a gangster movie.

Equally mysterious are Mom's beginnings with him. She was nineteen in 1964 and living in Vancouver, supposedly housekeeping for a wealthy Jewish family. Looking at old photos of her, I can see why my father noticed her right away. She was petite and beautiful, shy and unassuming with delicate features, neatly curled auburn hair and bright hazel eyes. They met at the Belmont Hotel downtown, and in no time at all he persuaded her to help him get rid of a suitcase filled with counterfeit twenties.

Mom never spoke about her past and I always wondered if she was working as a prostitute. The secrecy of her early life, not to mention the recollections of Aunty Sandra and Mom's best friend, Barb, has led me to believe this. It's difficult to fathom what would have seduced her into such a world, although I suspect it may have been heroin. I can only imagine the ugliness she must have endured and the shame and self-hatred she must have felt throughout her life. Even now, I feel as if I have betrayed her in writing this, but I must share her beginnings in order to share my own.

In looking at Mom's early life, many things don't make sense. Why she would end up on the street, using drugs? Her childhood seemed idyllic, my grandparents loving and kind.

Everyone knew her to be highly intelligent, an avid reader and writer of poetry. What is even more puzzling is that she was terribly shy, almost to the point of being an introvert, with little or no self-confidence. Aunty Sandra remembers her as somewhat sickly and depressed as a young woman, although the initial signs of lupus would only appear later, after my birth.

At first, I thought my father might have bought her from a pimp and had her working, but now I believe he rescued her despite the lifestyle he drew her into. He managed to get her off the streets and heroin and even paid for the burial of her first baby, which wasn't his and which died at birth.

My parents were married in Whonnock, B.C., (a little town close to Maple Ridge) in 1964 under an alias name and spent the next two years in hiding, moving from province to province every couple of months. Mom was surprised to find out that my father was already married and had a young daughter. In spite of this she stayed with him, and in 1965, while dodging the police in Port Alberni, she became pregnant with me. Not wanting to raise a baby on the run, she finally convinced him to turn himself over to the authorities. They returned to Maple Ridge where he turned himself in. Ironically, he ended up having a heart attack on the stand and beating most of his charges.

I was born in July of 1966, the very day my father stood trial. He was rushed to the same hospital for treatment. Though there were guards posted outside his room, Mom somehow managed to bring me to see him. After he recovered, he was sentenced to two years less a day for fraud and then sent to Oakalla prison.

I'm told my father saw me only twice after that, and in the visiting room at the prison he held and kissed me, marvelling at the new life that slept so soundly in his arms. I suppose if ever I felt close to him it was then, though I cannot remember him. As with so many other people, he has faded to that part of my memory where nothing exists but empty space, space that has become inaccessible over time.

Mom soon met up with her high-school sweetheart, Tommy. He had two young daughters and was unhappily married and, like Mom, wanted something better out of life. They began to date again and it wasn't long before they decided to run away together. Three months after my father went to jail, Tommy, Mom, and I moved to Hope, B.C. We lived there less than a year and then Tommy found a job in Lynn Lake, Manitoba. While Tommy made arrangements, Mom and I went to stay with Aunty Sandra and Uncle Tim in Washington.

I can only guess why Mom ran away with Tommy. Perhaps she feared my father wouldn't change and that our lives would be spent on the run from the police. Perhaps having me had changed her, had given her new hopes and dreams, a reason to leave behind the pain of the past.

We left Washington and took the train to Lynn Lake. Mom said that when Tommy met us at the train station he reminded her of an expectant father. He couldn't have been more happy to see us. He had rented a trailer in town, and Mom told me that she cried when she saw the nursery. He had spent hours painting and decorating it, filling it from top to bottom with toys and stuffed animals.

We lived in Lynn Lake less than a year. When Tommy's job at the lignite mine finished we moved to La Ronge, Saskatchewan, where he took a construction job which lasted only a couple of months. Then in 1968 we moved to Whitehorse in the Yukon. For Mom and Tommy it was a place where they could build a life together.

I don't know if Mom ever talked to my father before she left or if she just vanished without a word. Either way, I never saw him again, and he never once tried to contact us. When I was older she gave me two wedding pictures, and I recall feeling oddly angry at seeing my parents smiling and happy: my father standing tall and stiff in his black suit, his dark hair neatly greased and combed, his eyes black as crows and spying something beyond the camera, something that I desperately wanted to see but couldn't; and my mother, tiny and glowing in her crisp white dress, gloves, and veil, looking unused and untouched by any of the ugliness I would later come to know.

Looking at them now, I can only guess what my life might have been like had she waited for him, had *I* tried to find him. And yet, over the years, he has become more fiction than fact. Sometimes I look at myself in the mirror and wonder if I look like him. And I wonder if *he* ever thinks about me or imagines the many presents I might have given him on that special day, a day I have never celebrated..

Two

New Beginnings, Old Worlds Forgotten

I often wonder if the secrecy of Mom's life, even my own, began with the shame my grandfather carried throughout his life for being Métis. Perhaps it goes back even farther, back to his mother, my great-grandmother. It's painful to think that three generations — all of whom died before they were sixty — grew up in a world of half-truths and broken blood ties. And yet I have come to understand this secrecy. My spirit-keepers have refused to dismiss the truth and its carefully buried pain. I have always been hungry to unearth my grandfather's legacy, my mother's inheritance, no matter how poor or unworthy he felt it to be.

She was someone else's
dirty Cheechum story.
The manager probably said,
get that drunk squaw outta here
when they finally found her
stretched out cold
on the floor, by the bed
wearing her fox coat & boots
ready to go.

Years later
it was my grandmother who asked
how she died.
A broken heart, my Mooshoom said,
dismissing the topic as if
it wasn't his to begin with.

Cheechum: Great-grandmother
Mooshom: Grandfather

Like so many other things, the pieces of my grandfather's puzzle have come to me via letters from various relatives, marriage, birth and death certificates. Still, many remain lost or yet to be discovered. I have relied a great deal upon my grandmother's recollections, although much of my grandfather's childhood and past continues to be a mystery. The secrecy of his life is reflective of that time in Canadian history when there were few, if any, opportunities for those of mixed ancestry.

My great-great grandmother, who was known as Kohkum (Grandma) Otter, was a Cree woman whose ancestors probably came from Saskatchewan or Manitoba. Very little is known about her life or children although I suspect she was the "country wife" of a Hudson's Bay factor. Their daughter, great-grandmother Ida May, married Levis Scofield, from Aberdeen, South Dakota, with whom she had a family. They lived in Portage la Prairie, Manitoba, and as the story goes, they fought continally and were known as the "Battling Scofields." A short time later they separated and Levis moved back to the States and re-married. Great-grandmother Ida took up with a French half-breed farmhand and trapper, Johnny Custer, settled in Alonsa, Manitoba, and had my Grandfather Wilfred George and another girl and boy. In spite of her first marriage, the children were registered as Scofield, so their real father's lineage remains a mystery to this day.

Like most of the children of half-breed families in the 1920s, they grew up in poverty and shame. For that generation, there was little if anything to be proud of. Riel had been hanged less than a century earlier for his involvement with the Northwest Rebellion of 1885; his dreams of peace and equality were long since forgotten, and the Indian and Métis lands were sold off to homesteaders. Many of the families that had once been proud and strong, independent and hopeful, were now reduced to squatting on Crown Lands or living in shanty towns, outcasts in their own country.

Thus began a life of lies and secrecy for many mixed-blood people. Grandpa kept great-grandmother Ida a secret and refused to speak about her, at least not in front of others. He later told my grandmother that she died alone somewhere in northern Manitoba in a hotel room. He said that she died of a broken heart, but I can only guess at the circumstances, which I am certain weren't fair or just.

Grandpa left home at thirteen with a grade-three education and spent the next fifteen years riding the railcars across the country, working at whatever jobs he could find. He later found work on the road gangs with the CPR. Eventually he made his way to Prince Albert, Saskatchewan, where he met Avis Goud. It was an unusual match, crossing those invisible lines of race and class, which I am sure Grandpa was well aware of.

Grandma Avis's parents were among the first homesteaders in Estevan, Saskatchewan. Her mother, great-grandmother Brenzel, was Dutch and came from a large family who had roots in Pennsylvania, and her father, great-grandfather Goud, was a mixture of German and English, having immigrated with his parents to England from Germany as a boy. He came from a prominent family and was educated in private schools. In the 1800s he immigrated to Maine, USA, met my great-grand-mother and resettled in Saskatchewan, acquiring 650 acres of prime farmland.

Grandma Avis's childhood, of course, was very different from Grandpa's. She was raised with the Bible, literature, and art, taught to be elegant and refined. Like her brothers and sister, she finished high-school and went to college. She became an accountant, taking a job in Prince Albert with Canadian Airways, which mostly delivered mail and supplies to remote communities in the North. She was the first white woman to set foot at Cree Lake, and I doubt very much that she would have imagined marrying someone like my grandfather.

When she met Grandpa a short time later and they married, he never told her he was Native. By the standards of the day, they were both old to be getting married: Grandpa was thiry-four and Grandma was thirty-two. I suppose Grandpa felt that his chances were already limited and he didn't want to restrict them any further.

It seems odd to me that my grandmother would have never identified him as being Native. Although he was fair-skinned, he had dark eyes and hair, predominant Cree features. Perhaps she did know or suspect something, but chose to overlook it. She knew little about his family but recalled that he seldom saw his brother and sister, and when he did, they met in private. She said these meetings lasted for hours and that Grandpa would be quiet and withdrawn for days after. She always wondered about their secrecy but respected it.

At first, my grandparents' life was happy and stable. They came to Vancouver in 1943, and Grandpa worked at various construction jobs in northern B.C. In 1944 my mom, Dorothy, was born and two years later Aunty Sandra was born, at which time they acquired the homestead in Whonnock. Grandma traded her mink coat for the property and they had enough money to build a small house, buy some chickens, and put in a garden. They attended church every Sunday, and Grandpa, though he could barely read, became an elder of the church. They were well respected by the community and considered a generous, loving family.

Then things started to fall apart. Grandpa started having epileptic seizures. He had suffered from them as a boy, but they had disappeared as he got older. He never told Grandma — another secret — and so she knew nothing about them until after Aunty Sandra was born. When Aunty Teresa was born in 1953 she was a surprise to everyone, especially Grandma, who was already forty-six. With Grandpa's health getting worse, making it difficult to keep up the farm, Grandma went to work for a real estate agency in Maple Ridge. Then in 1956 they sold the farm and bought a house in town so that Grandma could be closer to work. Maple Ridge, although still relatively small, was a bustling city compared to the dirt roads, acres of wild bush, and the little farm community of Whonnock.

After my grandparents moved to town, Mom's childhood came to an abrupt end. Grandpa's seizures were coming almost daily and he wasn't able to work. In desperation, Grandma took a night job at a mink ranch, stretching and fleshing the hides. Mom and Aunty Sandra began to experience the first pangs of adolescence, trying hard to fit in with the other kids at school. Mom, who was normally shy and resigned, began to experiment with drugs, getting in with the wrong crowd. Aunty Sandra, who was now fourteen, met my uncle Tim and became pregnant.

I've talked with Aunty Sandra at great length about their early lives, trying to make sense of the misery Mom would later come to experience. Why did she end up on the street? Why did she wind up using heroin and meeting someone like my father? My grandparents, notably my grandfather, loved his girls more than anything in the world. To him, they could do no wrong. He never punished them or made them feel ugly or worthless and my grandmother was loving and kind, God-fearing and good-natured. Mom, Sandra, and Teresa didn't come from an abusive home, and yet their lives turned out to be filled with abuse and violence — everything my grandfather had escaped.

By the time Grandpa died of a massive brain hemorrhage in

1964, Mom had already met my father in Vancouver and Aunty Sandra was married with a two-year-old daughter. Teresa was eleven, and with Grandpa gone and Grandma working, she was suddenly all alone. Four years after Grandpa's death, Grandma remarried and sold the house, but her new husband was nothing at all like Grandpa. He was cheap and ill-tempered, even jealous of the girls. Teresa hated him and couldn't wait to leave home. She finally got married and moved to Washington where she began a family of her own.

I always regret never knowing my kind and generous grandfather, particularly as I had no father. Throughout my childhood Mom told me numerous stories about him. Like my aunts, she loved him a great deal and I loved him by extension. I often wonder how he felt holding Mom for the first time; if he saw great-grandmother Ida in her eyes or simply a new beginning, a chance to start over the way Mom would with me.

My grandparents' marriage of secrets provided a better life for my mom and aunts, at least as far as racism was concerned. Perhaps, for Grandpa, it was the only way to try to guarantee them fairness and dignity. And yet the price of his silence, the denial of his heritage, has left hundreds of unanswered questions and, I strongly believe, deeply affected each generation of my family. Little did I know that one day his silence would become the catalyst for my own self-acceptance, love, artistic expression, and ultimately, survival.

Three

Only the Memories Live Forever

The mam-tone-ne-yechee-kunna
spilled from her mouth
and trickled
in spurts, me a dry bed
thirsting achee-mowina.

La Ronge, Lynn Lake
were dots on a map
revisted by my finger.
The pee-peesis before me
floated around blue inside
and went silently with her
to the grave.

But Ke-wetinohk
I remember
Whitehorse
we lived in an old trailer
until the house was built.
The bush was our playground.
A team of huskies
pulled us kids around

kissing our snotty noses
where icicles hung.

ka-meyoskamik
the pups got sold.
At five
I developed a tendency
to whimper, howl
inconsolably.

---

mam-tone-ne-yechee-kunna: memories
achee-mowina: stories
pee-peesis: baby
Ke-wetinohk: North
ka-meyoskamik: springtime

My first memory is of the house being built in Whitehorse. I remember the smell of the freshly cut timber, the rhythmic pounding of the workers' hammers, their voices and laughter trickling down from the roof and filling the empty house and bush as if a radio had suddenly been turned on.

Our house was little more than a big shack, but it was ours. Leah, Tommy's youngest daughter, and I shared one room and slept on bunkbeds that Tommy built. The mattresses were thick green foam and on top of these Mom put old blankets. A toy-box and an old dresser stood below a small window at the back of the house. Mom and Tommy's room was next to ours and had a homemade bed, old dresser and two large steamer trunks. Like most of the house, the kitchen and dining room were unfinished. The kitchen had a gas stove, old fridge, plank shelves and open-faced cupboards for storing food and dishes. In the dining room was a heavy aborite table which sat under the window. The floors throughout were covered with white linoleum. The living room was the only room that was close to being finished, with two big windows that overlooked miles of bush, and an overstuffed couch and armchair, a coffee table, and end tables on which stood glass-shaded lamps. On the wall hung a large tapestry of a trapper racing through the snow with his dog team. On the back porch stood an old wringer washing machine and a metal washtub which we'd used as a bathtub before we got electricity and plumbing. In spite of its shortcomings, I loved that house.

Shortly after the house was built, Tommy got custody of Leah, and she came to live with us. I was too little to notice any difference and just accepted her as my sister. Leah was four years older than I, an awkward child with long stringy hair and sad brown eyes. She cried a lot and seldom left her father's sight. Mom spent a great deal of time holding and soothing her, and I recall feeling oddly jealous, becoming a cry-baby myself. It must have been hard for Mom and Tommy in those early months, making sure that we both felt equally loved.

We lived fifteen miles out of Whitehorse, which seemed like a big city, although it was a typically small northern town. There were clothing stores, hotels, and cafés on Main Street and it always seemed to be filled with activity, mostly people going in and out of the bars. There was an old log church in town and some older buildings that dated back to the gold rush. A Native handicraft store sold mukluks, moccasins, gloves, vests, jackets, and various sewing items. I still remember the smell of the smoked moosehide and the beautifully beaded designs on the clothing. Mom and Tommy each bought a pair of mukluks, and Mom bought me a muskrat pelt, which became my most treasured possession.

Tommy had a job at the copper mine and left for work every day at 4:00 a.m. In the summer it wasn't so bad because the sun never went down, but in the winter he had to leave two hours early. Most of the time Leah and I were still asleep, but sometimes I woke to find Mom busy at the stove, frying bacon and eggs, humming softly to herself. She loved the North and the remoteness of our lives, and like the kerosene heater, she was forever aglow in Tommy's presence. She took great pride in the house and worked tirelessly, scrubbing the floors, painting and decorating, whatever it took to make our home warm and cozy. Those times were the happiest of her life.

When Grandma and her new husband, Lyle, came to visit us our first summer in Whitehorse, I was so excited I followed her everywhere. With her powder and perfume, curled silver hair, rhinestone glasses, long colourful dresses and matching earrings, she was like a queen. They brought a small trailer that Grandma decorated with pictures, floral-print curtains and a matching bedspread. I would find any excuse to go there. Sometimes I even got to sleep with her and she would draw me pictures and tell me stories.

Lyle was a horrible man, cranky and impatient, especially when it came to us kids. Grandma would come huffing into the house, red-faced and threatening to leave him. Sure enough, towards the end of summer, Lyle packed up the trailer and left without her. She stayed with us for the winter and then in the spring she went home to Maple Ridge where she moved into an apartment. I cried for weeks after she left.

At some point Mom and Tommy decided they wanted to breed huskies, so they bought a blue-eyed bitch and a breed dog from a racer who lived a few miles down the road. They built a huge compound, and in no time there were cute little puppies running around. Leah and I were in heaven, playing and sleeping with our new babies, and many tears were shed at the very mention of selling them. Nevertheless, come springtime, the pups were sold, and after our fits had passed, we could barely wait for the next litter.

The winter carnivals in Whitehorse, called the Sourdough Rendezvous, were unlike anything I'd ever seen. Thousands of people came from all across the Yukon, Canada, and Alaska to race and show off their magnificent dog teams. Huskies everywhere were decorated with colourful pom-poms and tassels: all of them excited and barking, waiting their turn at the various competitions, one of which was to see how many pounds of flour or dog food a team could carry. Sometimes they even carried up to eight hundred pounds. The owners or "mushers" stood behind them cracking their whips and screaming, "Mush! Mush!" They looked like giants to me, with their long bushy beards, their parkas and fur caps, their mukluks and gloves.

The highlight of the carnival was the race, which usually lasted a couple of weeks along a course that covered hundreds of miles, ran through dense bush and snow, and had various check-in points along the way. Whoever made it to the finish line first was the winner and collected a huge cash prize. The ending was often dramatic, with two teams coming in at once and the crowd jumping up and down and screaming.

When Leah started grade four in the fall, Mom and I were alone during the day. My love of literature and music grew out of that time as she spent hours reading and playing old records for me. I remember sitting on her lap, singing along with Patti Page's "How Much Is That Doggy in the Window" and Wilf Carter's "Blue Canadian Rockies." She would hug and kiss me, laughing at the little stories I made up, forever telling me that I was her "special blessing." A deep bond developed between us.

But soon, Mom became very ill. Tommy did his best to look after us and keep the house in order. Mom was so sick that she could barely get out of bed in the morning, let alone get Leah off to school or tend to me. Her headaches were getting worse by the day, and she could hardly walk without help. Sometimes at night I woke to hear her crying, and I would sneak into their bedroom. Tommy would be holding and rocking her, talking softly. I was so scared I would burst into tears. Tommy would take me back to bed, lie down with me, and stroke my hair, promising that everything would be better tomorrow.

As Mom got worse, Tommy could barely keep up. His once-happy face was now drawn and tired, though he still pretended to be a good father and husband. Leah began to miss school and fell behind in her studies. She tried her best to look after me, telling me fantastical stories about faraway places. Then one day, without warning or even a goodbye, Mom was gone. Tommy wouldn't say where she was, though I kept asking. Nothing in my life made sense after she went away. I felt such a terrible loneliness, an emptiness comparable only to death. I remember very little except for the howling of the huskies, the long nights, and the frightening blackness that seemed to envelop my five-year-old world.

Four

The Birth of Shadows

The only real home I would ever know was falling apart around me. Tommy worked non-stop to keep things going until he could make other arrangements. Fortunately, his boss was understanding, and he would rush home on his breaks to fix us lunch and do the housework. As it was summertime, Leah was out of school (she had failed grade five due to missing so many days) and she looked after me until Tommy got home. But then one night he came home so tired and bedraggled that I was sure he, too, was sick and was going to die. After supper he pulled us to his lap and told us that we were going to be staying with a nice family who lived closer to town in a trailer park. Leah and I were hysterical. Once he calmed us down, he promised it wouldn't be for very long. He would see us often and soon everything would be back to normal. And so Leah and I were moved a few days later.

The Johnstons lived in an old dilapidated trailer that was filthy from top to bottom, filled with beat-up funiture that reeked of sour bodies and cat pee. Dirty dishes and bags of garbage were strewn everywhere, and the trailer swarmed with blackflies. The Johnstons had six kids, all of whom looked as dirty as the trailer. Their eldest daughter, who was the same age as Leah, tiptoed around as if she were walking on eggshells. She had big frightened eyes and looked as if she would suddenly burst into tears if someone looked at her the wrong way. Their other children varied in age from one to seven; some of them were still in diapers that sagged and smelled to high heaven. Mr. Johnston, a big burly man who looked as if he hadn't taken a bath or shaved in years, had yellow and chipped teeth and dirty clothes. He was quiet and seldom spoke more than two words. He came home after work, ate supper, and then plunked himself down in front of the TV until bedtime.

Mrs. Johnston was one of the meanest people I have ever known. Her thin red hair hung in greasy strings and her mammoth stomach and chest bounced when she walked. She was forever yelling at her kids, and everything that came out of her mouth began with "You fucking little bastard." She wouldn't just spank her kids but would hit them with closed fists or whatever else came in handy.

One instance shocked me so badly that for a long time, even in adulthood, I thought I had either made it up or dreamed it. It happened about a month after Leah and I came to stay with them, when Mr. Johnston was at work. Mrs. Johnston flew into a rage over something her eldest daughter had done. There was an old bed in the corner of the living room and above that was a large plant hook that had been screwed into the ceiling. Mrs. Johnston grabbed her daughter by the hair and slapped her across the face. She then tied her wrists together and forced her up on the bed, all the while yelling at her to fasten her wrists through the plant hook. The poor girl was screaming and begging, but her mother ripped the shirt off her back and began to beat her with a bullwhip. I'll never forget the sound of that whip tearing across her back and her awful screams. Leah and I were hysterical and ran outside. I have blocked the memory of what happened later. I remember only that it was evening and we were in the living room watching TV: Mr. and Mrs. Johnston on the couch, their kids rolling around on the floor like puppies, and that poor girl slumped in the corner, her eyes big and wild.

Tommy came to see us whenever he could, which wasn't nearly as often as we hoped. Sometimes weeks would go by, and when he did arrive, he seemed preoccupied and distant, almost as if he'd stopped loving us. I can recall vividly the sound of his truck pulling into the driveway and the excitement I felt at thinking maybe he would take us home. Leah and I clung to him. Most times he took us for ice cream, and in those few short hours, our lives would once again be happy and safe. We tried desperately to tell him what was happening, but he didn't seem to hear us. Instead, he would make us promise to do our best and mind our manners. Over time his visits grew less and less. At the end of each visit, he would promise to come for us, saying that soon, very soon, we would be together again.

Leah became my sole connection to anything loving and secure. Whenever she wasn't busy doing housework or school-work, she spent every available moment with me, protecting me whenever there was trouble. She held and rocked me in secret, telling me her fantastical stories and describing what our lives would be like as soon as Mommy and Daddy came to get us. Of course, Leah and I were not allowed to sleep together. I shared a bed with three other little ones and would wake up soaked from their pee. Each morning, before school, she would take me to the river and bathe me. She would smile and playfully say, "At least my baby brother knows how to use the potty." While Leah was at school, I usually played by myself or watched TV with the other kids. I was content wandering off down to the river where I would daydream or think about the stories Leah told me, sometimes making up my own. My stories were even more grand, filled with princes and monsters, kings and queens. Sometimes Mr. and Mrs. Johnston, their children, Leah, Tommy, and Mom were cast in my stories. Mrs. Johnston was always the witch and Mr. Johnston her helper. Their children had been stolen from a nice family and were being held captive in the forest. Tommy and Mom, the king and queen, sent out their guards to find them. After the witch and her helper were killed, the children were brought back to the castle where they lived happily ever after with Leah and me, the princess and prince.

Mrs. Johnston didn't like Leah, and it wasn't long before she started hitting her, too. At first, I tried to protect her, but Mrs. Johnston slapped me and told me go outside and play. I could hear Leah inside yelling at her never to hit me again. But that was followed by crashing and banging, and I knew she'd gotten a licking. Leah never once cried or begged.

Another afternoon, Leah was doing laundry and I was helping her. Mrs. Johnston had an old wringer washer like ours and I was fascinated by how the rollers worked. I was standing on a chair and feeding the clothes through, when all of a sudden my hand got caught. I panicked and started to scream. Mrs. Johnston came running into the kitchen, grabbed my hand and yanked it out. She threw me down and was about to kick me when Leah tackled her to the floor. Mrs. Johnston went down like a ton of bricks and, to my surprise, she didn't hit her. Instead, she calmly got up and said to Leah, "Next time, keep the little fucker's hands away from there!"

Mrs. Johnston left Leah alone after that, at least physically, but she did things to torment me. One afternoon, after the chores were done, Leah and I were sitting on the kitchen floor looking at the Sears catalogue. I was showing her all of the things I wanted for our dream home. Leah found a pair of scissors and we started cutting out the pictures and taping them on the wall. Mrs. Johnston came into the kitchen and flew into a rage. "What in the hell do you think you're doing!" she screamed, pushing me out of the way to look at our collage. She ripped the pictures down, grabbed my arm, and yanked me to my feet and started to shake me. "Get your hands off of him!" Leah screamed. "He's not doing anything wrong." Mrs. Johnston spun around and was about to slap Leah when she lunged at her with the scissors. "Don't ever touch him again, you bitch!" Leah screamed. Mrs. Johnston snatched the scissors out of her hand and slapped her across the face. She told us that we weren't allowed to talk to one another, and that if she caught us, we would wish we were dead.

The next few weeks were miserable. And then shortly before Christmas, Tommy came to get us — for good! Leah and I were so happy that we burst into tears. Mrs. Johnston hugged and kissed us, telling Tommy that we'd been no trouble at all. I remember looking over her huge shoulder and seeing her daughter cowering in the corner, looking as if she would give anything to come with us.

In spite of our newfound happiness, we didn't go home. To our great disappointment, Tommy had moved to a small two-bedroom trailer across town. It looked as lonely as we felt. It had ugly red shag carpets and dark-panelled walls, broken cupboards and closets, a gas stove, and a small oil-burning heater in the middle of the living room that smelled so bad it burned our eyes and gave us headaches.

Christmas that year was happy and yet terribly lonely. Mom was still gone. I was positive that she was dead for I hadn't been told otherwise, nor could I imagine why she would just leave us. Tommy bought a small tree and we decorated it, drinking mugs of hot cocoa and listening to Christmas carols on the radio. We clung to him as if he were a life-raft, and he sang "I'll Be Home for Christmas" and read us stories just the way Mom had. Christmas morning we got all sorts of presents and candy, but even though we were safe and with Tommy, I remember thinking that Santa didn't give me Mommy back because I was a bad boy, although I wasn't sure what I'd done.

After the holidays, Tommy went back to work and our lives were uprooted once again. When he made arrangements for us to stay with another work buddy, Leah and I panicked. How could he do this to us again? But all of our pleading and tears made no difference, and we were moved after the new year.

To our surprise and great relief, Audrey and Paul were nothing at all like the Johnstons. They were in their mid-twenties, newly married, living in town in a two-bedroom apartment. We adored Audrey, who wore bright fashionable clothes and jewellery, make-up and perfume just like Grandma. She fixed her hair in curlers and spent hours brushing it out, piling and pinning it neatly on top of her head. I thought Paul was the most handsome man I'd ever seen. He was tall and broad-shouldered, with messy blond hair and a rugged face that was forever rough with stubble. Once a week he played hockey and would come home smelling of sweat and old equipment. I always waited up for him, and as soon as he walked through the door, he would scoop me up and swing me around.

Our lives returned to normal. Leah went back to school and I started grade one. Audrey and Paul lived near the school and so every morning she would walk us there. School was the most wonderful place ever! We drew pictures, learned our ABCs, practised how to count and tell time. Best of all, the teacher read us a new story every day.

Finally, I felt safe. I wanted to stay with Audrey and Paul forever. Occasionally, Tommy came to see us, but more and more his visits meant nothing. Like Mom, he'd become a shadow and I wanted him to go away forever. Leah and I didn't need him any more. Paul was our daddy now, and Mom was dead, and Audrey was kind and pretty. We had a new home and family, and this time nothing could break us apart.

Five

A Merciless God

Before Mom left us, she taught Leah and me to say our prayers at bedtime. She would tuck us in and tell us to close our eyes and repeat after her, "Now I lay me down to sleep. I pray the Lord my soul to keep. If I should die before I wake, I pray the Lord my soul to take."

I didn't know who God was or what he even looked like. I had seen pictures in Grandma's Bible of a long-haired man dressed in a scarlet robe, surrounded by little children and sheep. Grandma told me that his name was Jesus and that he was the Son of God. I thought that God must look like him, only older. Leah said that he had a long white beard (I had visions of the mushers) and that he answered prayers — something I thought to be wishes.

While we were at the Johnstons, Leah and I said our prayers faithfully, meeting secretly every night, whispering them in the safety of the washroom or hallway. Afterwards, she held and kissed me, reassuring me that God would keep us safe. Sometimes when the pain was great Leah would whisper in my ear, "Shh, don't cry. God sees everything. Mommy and Daddy will be back soon. Maybe tomorrow we'll go home and play with our puppies." Each day I waited for the white-bearded musher to come and save us.

In July, I had my sixth birthday. I was so happy that I didn't give Mom or Tommy a second thought. Audrey decorated the apartment with balloons and streamers and baked a chocolate cake which she covered with minature hockey players. I got all sorts of gifts, but best of all was the little hockey stick that Paul gave me. That day I made my first career decision — I wanted to be a hockey player, just like Paul.

Summer was soon over and Leah and I were happily preparing for school when one Sunday, Tommy came to get us. How I hated him! And how I hated God! Our prayers had been answered too late. I didn't need my parents now. I had Audrey and Paul and Leah. Audrey started to cry and began to pack our things. Paul was in the living room, sitting in his recliner, looking dazed and angry. When he didn't do anything I became frantic. I threw myself in his lap, sobbing, "I don't wanna go! I wanna stay here with you and Audrey! Please, I don't wanna go! Please!"

It was the first time in my life I had ever seen a grown man cry. After our things were packed and waiting by the door, Tommy thanked Paul and handed him an envelope. Without a word, he shoved it back into Tommy's hand, looking as if he wanted to hit him. He went to the hallway closet and took out my hockey stick, handed it to me, and said, "Be good, little guy. I'll see you on the rink, okay?" Audrey held us close and kissed our tears away, making Tommy promise to bring us over often.

Tommy had rented an apartment in the same building as Audrey and Paul, but it wasn't the same. Unpacked boxes were piled everywhere. There were no pictures on the wall, and the furniture was crammed into the middle of the living room. Although there were things that I recognized, nothing felt like home — not like the home I remembered. Tommy, too, was different. He seemed like a robot: methodical, moving towards something I could neither see nor understand. He tried to hold and kiss me, but it felt half-hearted. He didn't even take us to see Audrey and Paul.

When Grandma arrived a few weeks later, I was so excited. At last, I thought, there would be some order to our lives. But instead of unpacking the boxes and organizing the apartment, she began to pack even more. When Tommy was home, Grandma seldom spoke to him, and she, too, seemed to be in a world of her own.

Then one morning, after Leah had gone to school, Grandma took me to the airport. It was a cold, late autumn day, and from the back of the taxi window I remember watching the leaves break from the trees and set sail on the wind like tiny brown kites. Grandma explained that we were going on a special holiday, and that I was going to be staying with her. When I asked about Tommy and Leah, she grew silent, smiled, and then kissed me.

I was so excited about being on a plane that I completely forgot about everything. We were flying up to heaven, to where God and Mom lived. I pressed my face to the window and saw the river snaking its way through Miles Canyon, the endless snow-covered trees, and the fluffy clouds where angels slept at night. After we landed in Vancouver, I realized for the first time that Tommy and Leah were really gone. Grandma did her best to console me, assuring me that I would soon see them, but deep down, I knew it was a lie. They were gone just like Mom, and I would never see them again.

That day I retreated to a silent place within, a place where God didn't live, where promises and prayers never came true, and where happiness and safety were a memory of the past.

Although I didn't know it at the time, Tommy was involved in a new relationship. All those months that Leah and I suffered his silence, he was beginning a new life. He never once told us of his plans or even where Mom had gone. Years later I would discover she had been sent to a psychiatric hospital in Edmonton, her first symptoms of lupus having been misdiagnosed as a mental illness. As with my father, I never saw Tommy again.

When I met Leah many years later, like so many other people, she was a total stranger to me.

Six

Refuge in Silence

"But Grandma," I protested, "I don't wanna live with Aunty Sandra and Uncle Tim. I wanna stay here with you."

"I know, honey. But you can't. Grandma's too old to look after you. Besides, don't you want to see Todd and Lisa?"

I couldn't understand why I had to go to Washington. More so, I couldn't understand why Grandma, too, was going to abandon me. I wanted Tommy and Leah. I didn't want to be on holidays any more. *I wanted to go home!*

But the following weekend, Uncle Tim came to get me. After Grandma hugged and kissed me, she gave Uncle Tim a box of my clothes, some sandwiches, and soda for the trip. Although it was only a three-hour drive from Grandma's, it seemed like the other side of the world. Aunty Sandra was excited about getting me, and she had fixed up a nice bedroom. After dinner she unpacked my things, most of which she threw out, as I'd outgrown them. Although we had grown up together, my cousins Todd and Lisa stood in the doorway, looking on curiously as if I was a total stranger.

I could see we wouldn't be friends. Lisa was three years older and nothing at all like Leah. She was quiet and watchful. She spent a great deal of time alone in her room, and she made me promise never to go in there unless I asked. Todd, who was the

28

same age as I, was rough and tumble. He played sports and had scabs on his elbows and knees. He was jealous of the attention his mother gave me and would purposefully do things to hurt me. Because I was shy and nervous, he would find any reason to play-fight. His "games" often left me in tears.

By now I believed I would never see Tommy or Leah again. Even Grandma was a stranger. Aunty Sandra and Uncle Tim were good to me, but it wasn't the same as having my own family. I knew that Aunty Sandra loved me a great deal, and over time we became extremely close. Uncle Tim worked out of town and was seldom home. When he was home, he drank a lot and he would push Aunty Sandra around. I missed my own mother and hoped desperately that she was still alive.

School saved me. I started grade three in the fall and once again found great joy in losing myself in picture books and stories. In the school library I spent hours poring over books on Indians. I was somehow drawn to them: their stately faces that looked so ancient and wise, their once-free life of travelling across the country by horse or canoe. I wasn't certain why, but I seemed to find something of myself in those books.

Aunty Sandra enrolled me, along with Todd, in sports. I begged her not to make me do it, but she insisted it would be good for me. More than anything, I wanted to read books and draw pictures. I was happiest wandering off into the forest or hiding in the treetops, imagining myself to be a Great Chief dressed in a long-feathered warbonnet and buckskin shirt.

Before I knew it, an entire year had gone by. So much had happened that it seemed as if I'd always lived there. I had settled into the family. Todd and Lisa had become more like my siblings and Aunty Sandra was more like my mother. Though I loved Uncle Tim, I remember being afraid of him much as I had been with Mrs. Johnston.

Then one day something extraordinary happened. It was a beautiful spring afternoon and I was outside playing when Aunty

Sandra called me in. "It's for you," she said, handing me the phone. Upon hearing the voice on the other end, I felt the blood rush to my head.

"Hello, darling," the voice said. "It's Mommy." I was so astounded I couldn't speak. "Darling," she continued, "I've thought about you every day. I love you more than anything in the whole wide world. Uncle Tim is coming to get me. I'll see you in a couple of weeks."

Hearing her voice that day was like being left in the middle of a desert without water. I wasn't sure if it had actually happened or if I had dreamed it, as I'd done so many times in the past. And now she was coming to see me.

The next few weeks were unbearable. I tried desperately to remember Mom's face, but instead I saw only Leah. Why could I remember everything so clearly — Tommy and Leah, the house in Whitehorse, the Johnstons, Audrey and Paul, even my grade-one teacher, but not her? I asked Aunty Sandra over and over if Mom had really called. I just couldn't understand how after all this time she could be alive.

Uncle Tim and Grandma drove two thousand miles to Edmonton to get Mom out of the psychiatric hospital. It was a late summer afternoon when they arrived back. I stood in the doorway and watched as the car pulled into the driveway. I felt as if I were dreaming, seeing everything in slow motion. Mom was small and frail-looking. Her hair was cut short and she wore glasses, a cowboy shirt, jeans, and flip-flops. I studied her for a few moments, trying to remember her, and then like a bursting dam, I ran to her. I threw myself in her arms and began to sob uncontrollably, the years of silence and separation finally coming to the surface. Mom was crying, too, and held me as if she'd never let go. She planted my face with kisses and wiped away my tears, promising to never leave me again. At last God had answered my prayers.

Mom and I returned to Maple Ridge a couple of weeks later. We moved into the Fraser Valley Hotel and lived there until she was able to find an apartment, a small one-bedroom suite in a big old building down by the river, which had a less-than-upstanding reputation. The suites were small and the walls were thrashed from years of neglect and smoking. Our suite was on the first floor and faced the courtyard which looked more like a garbage dump than a tranquil garden. On each side of the building was a long flight of stairs leading to the second floor where the suites were even smaller. There were also suites around the back and some of them had broken windows covered over with plastic or cardboard. But the rent was cheap and, from all inward appearances, it didn't seem too bad. A lot of single mothers on welfare lived there, as well as numerous alcoholics and drug addicts. Across the street, in another ramshackle building, lived the bootlegger, whom everyone called Fat Paul. His prices were exorbitant and it was rumoured that he pissed or spit in the bottles. Nevertheless, Fat Paul was never short of customers, Mom being one of them.

Mom tried her best to pick up our lives where we'd left off. But she was a stranger to me. She seldom smiled or laughed. Her words were slow and laborious, her movements methodical, as if she had only half her spirit. At night she would sit for hours, drinking and staring out the window, looking pensive and lost, as if trying to remember where she'd left something.

I couldn't understand why she had changed, but I knew something was terribly wrong. Her memory of the past and our lives in Whitehorse was completely gone. Years later, I discovered she'd undergone over seventy shock treatments while hospitalized in Edmonton. At one point she didn't even remember having me. The doctors and social workers tried to convince her to adopt me out, telling her that I deserved a much more stable life. But, as she said, "God saved her," and she refused to sign their papers.

I can't remember exactly when
the taste started
only that it came
one night
she grabbed her coat,
told me to wait.

The last time
I hollered, made such a fuss
this time
I wound up tagging along.

Hand in hand
we set out,
down the hill
past the bootlegger's shack,
my hungry eyes
spying for the first time
lonesome alleys, phantom dogs
on midnight streets.

After dark, she said
always walk
in the middle of the road.
And never,
ever get into cars.

Outside the hotel
safely tucked
behind the dumpster
she told me
count to a hundred.
Don't go anywhere,
don't talk to anyone —
just wait.

81, 82, 83
my black bear mother
slight as deer, soft as rabbit
toting her six-pack
slipped into my hand
the salmon jerky treat.

At first, I felt hopeful that we would find the happiness we'd known in Whitehorse. But little by little, my hopes gave way to reality. Mom began drinking more and more, often charging up bottles from Fat Paul until welfare cheque day. I felt it was my duty to make things better, and I sat up at night worrying, listening to her cry. In the mornings, while she slept, I scrubbed the apartment until it sparkled. My reward, of course, was to see her happy, if only for a couple of hours.

Then one day, when Mom's social worker came by, she got quite nervous and told me to go outside and play. But the worker wanted me to stay. She asked Mom all sorts of questions, things to do with medical forms and school registration. She asked if we had enough food, or if I needed any clothes. Then she started to ask me questions directly.

"Do you like it here, dear?"

"Yes," I mumbled, taking an instant dislike to her.

"Have you made any friends?"

"No." She gave me a puzzled look and I knew immediately it wasn't the right answer.

"Is that so," she inquired. "Don't you like to play?"

"Yes," I mumbled, this time keeping my eyes on the floor. I didn't want to get Mom in trouble. Then Mom jumped up from the couch and I was sure that she was going to hit her. The worker calmly smiled and then excused me.

I am not sure what happened that afternoon, but Mom was completely depressed when I came home. Later, I overheard her talking to Grandma on the telephone. She said someone had reported her to the welfare office and that she had to go into a treatment centre. Summer vacation was almost over and I was to be starting school in a couple of weeks. I was petrified of going to a new school and frightened by the thought of Mom leaving again. She tried to be encouraging, shopping for school supplies and new clothes, but deep down her heart wasn't in it. Arrangements had been made for her to go into treatment at the beginning of September. Grandma was to look after me, and despite the fear I felt about Mom leaving, I was relieved that Grandma was coming to stay.

Everything happened all at once. I started school a couple of days after Mom left. When Grandma said that we couldn't see or talk to her for a month, my heart sank. It seemed like an eternity. But I soon stopped worrying and lost myself in the routine of school. Once again, I loved it. I even made some new friends, although I was leery of getting too close to them, afraid that they would find out about Mom and me living in the slums on welfare.

I had one friend who knew the truth: the building manager's daughter. Abby was in the same class as me and had a real taste for trouble. She had a smart mouth and swore like a trooper. Like me, Abby didn't have a father and her mother was on welfare even though she managed the building. Because of her mother, she knew everyone's business and often made comments about the tenants while we were playing. She had a pale and sickly looking younger brother named Billy, whom she was forever picking on. Her mother was rough-looking and had an equally dirty mouth. Grandma called them "poor white trash," but I never repeated it. She was the only real friend I had.

Abby and I never played together at school, only after we got home. It was a private friendship, a secret fuelled by our shared poverty and its humiliating shame. For the most part, at school we completely ignored one another. We would exchange glances in the hallway or school yard, knowing full well that we had the power to destroy one another. Yet once we were home, we were inseparable.

Abby and I usually met a good mile from school and would walk the rest of the way home together. One afternoon, as we were approaching the building, I heard a woman singing an Indian song. I immediately stopped. As I looked up, I saw an Indian woman leaning out her bedroom window. "Hey, you kids," she called down, her words thick and slurred. "What did you learn at school today?"

"Never mind her," Abby groaned, grabbing my arm. "My mom told me not to talk to Indians. They're all drunks, you know."

I recall feeling angry at what Abby said, but also strangely embarrassed, as if she'd attacked me personally. That night, I thought about the Indian woman who lived on the second floor. She seemed so lonesome to me, I wanted to go back and talk to her, apologize for Abby's rudeness. But then I thought about Mom. I started to miss her more than ever, feeling as if I'd never see her again. Suddenly everything seemed hopeless: the ugly building where we lived, the Indian woman whose sad song echoed inside my head, even Abby, who in a matter of seconds had become more of an enemy than a friend.

I lay awake for a long time, pondering a world that made no sense at all. Why did God give some people more than others? Why didn't He give me a nice home and a happy family like the other kids at school? Why did I have to feel ashamed about the things I didn't cause? Why did I have a voice when no one ever seemed to hear me?

Seven

Ta-pa-koo-Me-way-win (Making Relations)

It was the same moon
glowing hot
from my aunty's mouth
while drinking.
Those demon fire-balls
bounced in my head
and became stories.
Mornings
I thought I heard them
rumbling her guts
behind the bathroom door.

Years later
I met others downtown,
all piss-moon talkers.
The yellow lines
dividing the road
said which side
we belonged on.
The alley or ditch
was where we pissed,
all swapping coyote scents,

charming
the scarred moon face
out of her
shameful silence.

Haw, ne-kis-key-sin

the language was spoken,
always spoken.

Ekwa ekose ke-toh-ta!

———————

Haw, ne-kis-key-sin: Now, I remember
Ekwa ekose ke-toh-ta: And so, listen

Mom got out of treatment two months later, and for the first time since coming back to Maple Ridge, she seemed happy. She started going to AA and began to meet all kinds of people, most of whom were recovering alcoholics with one common purpose: to stay sober. Sometimes she took me along to meetings, and I'd hear stories about them losing their homes, partners, and children. It was so depressing, and I wondered if any of them had lived in our building.

Abby and I continued to play together in spite of the hurtful things she said. When our regular games of hide-and-seek, river combing, and sitting in our old rusted jalopies grew boring, she got the idea to sneak around people's suites in the hopes of catching them at something — what, I didn't know, but it seemed thrilling at the time. One afternoon we were snooping around the back of the building when suddenly Abby grabbed my arm and hushed me. "Ho-ly fuck!" she burst out, pointing to one of the suites where the drapes were open. "That guy's playing with his dink." I was so shocked, I couldn't speak. Abby was grinning from ear to ear and she had a terrible twinkle in her eyes.

"Let's bang on his door and run away," she exclaimed gleefully.

"No," I said, disgusted that she would even suggest it.

"Oh, come on," she coaxed. "You're such a chicken shit."

Before I knew it, we crept to his front door, knocked loudly, and took off. As if that wasn't enough, Abby insisted we do it again. Only the second time, we got caught. The man threw open the door and stood there completely naked. He invited us in and Abby pulled me inside. He wanted us to take our clothes off and asked me to lie on top of Abby. He said he would give us each twenty dollars (which seemed like a lot of money) and made us promise not to tell anyone. Abby started to giggle and told him we were too young to fuck. I was so mortified I bolted out the door and ran home. A few moments later Abby came to get me, laughing so hard tears were streaming down her face. But later on we told her mother who immediately called the police. The man was arrested, and we never saw him again.

In spite of the severe warning we received from our mothers not to talk to anyone in the building, Abby and I continued to visit the tenants we knew. One tenant in particular was a retired teacher named Phil, whom our mothers trusted implicitly and whom we called Uncle Phil. He often took us to the lake or out for ice cream, and sometimes we even slept overnight. Uncle Phil didn't have any children of his own, and so our mothers encouraged us to spend time with him. He was loving and gentle, and treated us like nieces and nephews. But after a while he started to change. He would slip his hands down our swim trunks or ask us to sit in his lap and rock back and forth. We didn't tell our mothers for fear of breaking our promise to him. But then one night Billy came home crying, saying that Uncle Phil had tried to suck his penis.

I'll never forget the utter chaos of that night. Abby's mother woke Mom up and they stormed upstairs to Uncle Phil's and dragged him out of his apartment. They yelled and hit him as if they were going to kill him. The entire building was awake and everyone was watching. After the police came, and we were questioned, Uncle Phil was taken away. I remember watching him being escorted down the stairs and into the car, his hysterical sobs filling my ears like sharp knives. Abby, Billy, and I were told: "*Never talk to anyone in the building again.*" Mom then warned me she didn't want me playing with Abby any more, which made no difference because a short time later Abby's mother got back with her father. She quit her job, they left town, and I never saw Abby again.

With Abby gone, bad as she was, I didn't have a friend in the world. I wasn't interested in anyone at school, nor was anyone interested in me. I was just as happy to be alone, wandering off down to the river or losing myself in books. To me, no one could be as interesting as watching the river flow by with its massive log booms or reading about the great chiefs like Sitting Bull, Red Cloud, Geronimo, and Chief Joseph.

One afternoon, on the way home from school, I remembered the Indian woman. I hadn't seen her and wondered if maybe she had moved. I rushed home, threw my schoolbooks down and was already halfway up the stairs to her suite when I remembered Abby's words, "Indians are all drunks." I also remembered Mom's warning, but I had to know if she was still there. I crept around to her living-room window and sure enough she was busy at her sewing machine. She must have felt me watching her because she suddenly turned around. I froze on the spot. She came to the door, opened it, and looked at me inquisitively.

"You're Dorothy's boy, uh?" she asked, squinting through her glasses.

"Yes," I nodded, feeling ashamed for spying on her.

"Ah, den how's your mama?"

"Fine." She caught me looking into her suite and smiled.

"I'm jist doin' some sewing in here," she said. "Dis guy wants his slacks hemmed up. You wanna come inside?"

"I'm not supposed to," I said feebly. "My mom told me not to talk to anyone."

She looked at me thoughtfully, nodding her head. "Well, in dat case maybe it's not a good idea," she concluded. "Maybe first ask your mama, den you can come back to visit."

"Okay," I mumbled and shot off down the stairs before she even had a chance to close her door.

Oddly enough, I wasn't sure if she was even an Indian. She didn't really look like one, not like the Indians in my picture books. She had shoulder-length auburn hair which she wore tied back in a ponytail and had a small, narrow face with sharp features and light brown eyes. She wore large-framed glasses, a pink jogging suit, and matching slippers. She sort of looked like Mom, only older. But she talked funny, pronouncing her *t*'s as *d*'s, and I thought she might be from Europe — maybe even Italy.

That night I told Mom about meeting her. At first she didn't have a clue who she was, but then she suddenly remembered. "Oh, yes! That's Georgie. I've spoken to her in the laundry room. She seems like a very nice lady."

"Can I visit her then?" I asked hopefully.

"Only if you promise not to make a nuisance of yourself."

I was so excited, I could barely sleep. The next day, after school, I ran home and went straight up to see Georgie. When I peeked in the window she was busy at the sewing machine. I tapped on the glass and she came to the door.

"So you come back to visit me, uh?" she said. "You ask your mama?"

"Yes."

"Well den, *ke-pe-tah-kway*," she said, gesturing me inside. What language was that? I wondered.

Her suite was small and immaculate, smelling of pine-sol and freshly baked bread. The furniture was old and tattered, but it gleamed in the sunshine. There were piles of clothes, all neatly folded in baskets by the sewing machine. In one corner of the living room were stacks of old records, a stereo, and a guitar. A homemade quilt and richly coloured pillows covered the couch. In another corner stood or sat dolls of various sizes and shapes, all of them dressed in old-fashioned clothes and wearing miniature moccasins. Above the dining-room table hung pictures of the Virgin Mary and of a dark-haired man, smiling tenderly in a beaded picture frame.

"Dat's my boy, Danny," she said, pointing to the picture. "He's not wit us any more." I wasn't sure if that meant he was dead, but she looked sad and I didn't want to pry.

"What about school today?" she asked, changing the subject.

"It was okay."

"I bet you got all gold stars, uh?"

"That's only in kindergarten!" I laughed.

"Is dat so!" she teased, grinning through her glasses. "I taught maybe you were only tree years olt."

"I'm almost eight!" I exclaimed, grinning at her silliness.

"But not too olt for milk and cookies, I bet!" She went to the kitchen and started to fix me a plate. Her back was to me, and without thinking I suddenly blurted out my question: "Are you an Indian?"

"Sure," she said, turning around and smiling. "I'm a Cree — a *Nay-he-yow*!"

"Who?"

"A *Nay-he-yow*," she said, slowly pronouncing the word. "Dat means a Cree Indian. And what about you?" she asked.

I shrugged my shoulders, suddenly aware that I didn't know anything about my background.

"Well, den let's see," she said, coming over to look at me. "Hmm," she began, bending down to examine my face. "You got grey iyz and light hair, but you also got a big nose, high cheekbones, and big fat lips." I felt my face going red and she started to laugh. "I tink you must be an *Awp-pee-tow-koosan*, like me," she concluded. "I see it, too, in your mama."

"What's that?"

"Dat's a half-breed. Half dis and half dat."

"Half what?" I asked, afraid of the answer.

"You know, half devil and half angel," she teased.

"I don't think so," I politely answered. "I think I'm a great chief like Sitting Bull and Red Cloud."

"Is dat so!" she called out, looking at me closely, a smile breaking across her lips. "Oh, yes, now I can see it."

I sat back proudly on the couch and dug into the milk and cookies, pondering what she had just said about being a half-breed.

"But I heard you singing an Indian song," I suddenly blurted. She thought for a moment and then said, "Oh, yeah. My mudder taught me dat song. She was da *Nay-he-yow* and my fadder, he was French. I can sing in French, too!" she exclaimed proudly, rolling her *r* drastically.

Georgie was smart and funny, kind and wise, and I spent every available moment I had with her. She had lost all three of her children, two of them as babies to pneumonia, and Danny when he was thirty-three. He was coming home from Alberta for Christmas and was killed in a car accident. She seldom talked about her first two sons, but she talked about Danny all the time. She told me that he was a wonderful musician and that he knew how to play and sing every Hank Williams song. He was also a gifted artist, and sometimes she brought out his drawings to show me. I remember looking at them and touching them as if they were fragile, as if I were beholding a piece of him.

Sometimes, when I stayed overnight with Georgie, she told me stories about her childhood in northern Alberta, and how her mother had taught her to hunt and trap. She told me stories about the convent school she attended, the nuns and priests, and all of the mischief she and her chum Agnes got into. I spent hours at her table, wide-eyed and curious, drinking mugs of hot tea (she said tea was the only good thing to ever come out of

England), while she transported me to another time and place. My favourite stories were the ones about *We-sak-e-jack*, the First Man, the Trickster, and how he forever tried to trick the birds and animals. She also told me about *We-tik-koow*, the cannibal monster who roamed in the bush at night, looking for unsuspecting children to eat. Sometimes she would be doing beadwork or making a beautiful pair of moccasins or vest for someone. Her floral patterns and brightly-coloured beads were the most exquisite things I'd ever seen. In time, she taught me to do beadwork, giving me a little piece of moosehide to practise on. We sewed for hours on end, over tea and stories, and I gradually became a skilled beadworker. I recall how satisfied I felt finishing my very first pair of moccasins. She said that my work was much better than a lot of the old ladies back home, and her praise made me feel all the more special.

But there were also times when I wasn't allowed to see Georgie. Mom would say that she was busy and not to bother her, although I knew the truth. The drapes would be drawn and everything looked dark. Sometimes I could hear strains of the Carter Family or Hank Williams coming from her suite. Other times I would see her leaning out her bedroom window and she would call down, "How's my boy doing?" I knew she was drinking. I always felt sad when I saw her drunk, because I knew she missed Danny.

I never told Mom that Georgie called us half-breeds. I still wasn't sure what it actually meant, only that we were sort-of-Indians. But I told her everything else Georgie said and taught me. Mom never said much, only that she liked her a great deal and that she was happy I'd found such a good friend. And as always, she made me promise not to make a nuisance of myself.

A short time later, Georgie verbally adopted me in the Indian way, and from then on I called her *Ne-ma-sis* (my little mother; Aunty). She said the Creator had sent me to her and that I was meant to take the place of Danny. By now Mom and Georgie had become friends, and Mom was pleased to share me with her. Aunty began to teach me Cree, and I picked it up quickly, as if I'd heard it before, as if the words were buried somewhere within me. She taught me about the old-time medicines: how to prepare and use them, what their names were in Cree, the need to be quiet and respectful when I used them. The medicines, like *che-stay-maw* (tobacco) and *we-ke-mah-kah-sekun* (willow fungus) were used for "smudging" or praying, while the medicines like *muskeeg-ke-wapoy* (muskeg tea) and *a-cha-cha-moon* (sneezing root) were ground up and boiled into a strong tea and used for various ailments such as colds or fevers. And she told me about *Ke-chee-manitow*, the Creator, explaining that the Indian religion was the same as Christianity, and that the white people had no business telling the Indians how to pray; that they did so because they were afraid of what they couldn't see or understand.

The more Aunty taught me about the medicines and the old-time ways, the more I felt connected to something. I felt as if she had given me special knowledge that none of the other kids at school had. I felt a new and powerful connection with God, *Ke-chee-manitow*, who, unlike Grandma's Bible pictures, became the Great Spirit without a face: the Spirit that lived in the river and trees, mountains and rocks.

Mom seemed happy. She met someone at an AA meeting and began to date him. His name was Don and he lived in our building. He was tall and slim, had black hair and eyes, and he seemed like a nice man. Mom was head over heels for him and she acted like a schoolgirl, laughing and giggling. She started wearing make-up and jewellery, nice clothes, and even traded in her flip-flops for high heels.

At first I liked Don because he treated me kindly and listened to all of my Indian stories. He laughed and said I had a great imagination. I couldn't understand what he found so funny, because he was obviously part Indian. I wasn't sure about me or

Mom, but I figured we must be Indians — like Aunty — she had said so. Then one day when Don and I were alone in my room, I showed him some of the medicines Aunty gave me. He seemed uncomfortable and impatient. I assumed he would be interested, and without giving it a second thought, I said, "But you're an Indian." His face went about twenty shades of red. He grabbed my arm and squeezed it so tightly, I began to cry. "Don't ever fucking call me that again!" he hissed. He let go of me and went upstairs to see Mom. I was stunned by his response. I didn't tell Mom for fear of being called a liar or, worse yet, spoiling her newfound happiness.

Mom and Don continued dating and attending meetings together. By now he was having dinner with us and spending the night. Secretly I hoped he would go away, but he only seemed to come around more and more. I spent as much time as possible with Aunty, and told her what Don had done. "Dat bastard!" she roared. "You come stay wit Aunty whenever you want, my boy."

Now Don made no attempt to hide his dislike for me. I often overheard him talking to Mom, telling her I was spoiled, and that if she wasn't careful, I'd turn out to be one of those "poofters." I had no idea what that meant, but it sounded bad. He also told her that I was jealous of him and that I would do anything to split them up. He said that I needed strong but *loving* discipline, and to my surprise, Mom believed him. She turned the discipline over to him, and he used every opportunity to "show me the right way."

In the beginning Don would march me downstairs, force me to pull my pants down, and spank me. But then he started to use belts or whatever else he could find, like coat hangers or pieces of wood. Still, when that wasn't enough, he would hit me in the face or stomach. Sometimes he even threw me down the stairs. He would march down after me, grab me by the scruff of the neck, and shake me until I went limp. Mom knew he was getting carried away and tried to stop him, but he would hit her, too, all the while screaming, "Do you want a God damn brat on your hands!"

I had bruises and marks all over my body, and the teacher began to ask me questions. I always lied, telling her that I'd slipped or fallen. Once, when she asked me outright if someone was hitting me, I looked her straight in the eye and said no. Mom's social worker also came by, but nothing came of it. As usual, I stuck to my story, more for Mom than anything. I just couldn't bear to leave her again.

The only one who knew the truth was Aunty. How I loved and trusted her, even more than Mom! After my "punishments," I'd run up to her place and bury my face in her lap and cry. "Never mind, my boy," she'd soothe. "One day you'll show dat bastard whose boss — if not wit a good licking, den in udder ways."

Then came the blackest day. Mom announced that she and Don were getting married. I was so panic-stricken, I couldn't see straight. How could she? He hit her! He hit me! But she was determined and promised me he would change. All I had to do was behave and mind my manners. Everything, or so she wanted to believe, would turn out just fine. Later, Don sat me down and told me the new rules:

1. No more Indian stuff in the house.
2. No more sassing him or giving him dirty looks.
3. No more asking Mom for favours like staying up late to watch TV or read, I was to go directly to him.
4. No more wasting time after school, I was to come home every day and do my chores and homework.
5. No more Aunty.

Even before he got to the last rule I knew what it would be. He knew that I loved Aunty more than anything in the world and that I went to her whenever I had problems. I looked to Mom for help, but she looked away. After Don excused me, I ran as fast as I could down to the river where I sat and watched the murky water. I felt betrayed, as if my heart had been yanked out, as if a vital part of me had been killed. For the very first time I thought about my father and wished he was with me. Like Mom, I didn't know if I should love or hate him. But it was clear I hated Don. *Ke-chee-manitow* had given me Aunty — and now the Devil was taking her away.

Eight

Storms to Come

He stole the sun,
spoke thunder
coming down the mountain
only too proud
to swallow the last rays.

Like raven
he kept any warmth
sealed tight
in a box.
Never ask or beg
she said, her eyes
loose hinges
on a swinging door.

I knew then
not all storms
were good.

Aunty confirmed that Don was part Native. She told me that she had met him on the street one time, and because they were neighbours, she invited him over. He agreed and the next day over coffee, she asked him what tribe he came from. He got angry and told her he was a Black Scot and God damn proud of it! He huffed off and refused to speak to her again. "Dem are da worse kinda Indians," she told me. "Apples! Red on da outside and white on da inside."

Don was a recovering alcoholic and had been sober for three years. Aunty said when he first moved into the building, he was a big drunk like everyone else. But then he found AA, got a decent paying job, and went off welfare. It was a mystery why he hadn't moved, but for Mom and me, an ill-fated stroke of misfortune.

His daughter Sherry was five years older than I was and lived in northern B.C. with her mother (whom Don hated) and step-father. She worshipped her dad and thought he could do no wrong. Mom spent hours on the phone with her and they became extremely close. When she came down to visit us over the summer holidays I remember taking a quick dislike to her. It wasn't that she treated me badly, but I couldn't believe how blind she was when it came to her father.

Mom and Don got married in August before Sherry went home. Everyone was happy but me. I felt as if Mom and I were standing at the edge of a cliff, looking at the jagged rocks below, only she was oblivious to the stranger standing behind us. When I tried to warn Grandma, she told me not to cause any problems. It seemed so unreal. Mom and I were in terrible danger and no one cared — not even Grandma!

In spite of Don's rules and the severe beatings I knew I would get, I continued to see Aunty. She was the only one I trusted, and for an hour or so I could feel safe. I made sure to be home before Don got off work and hurriedly did my chores and home-work. Mom knew that I was seeing her, but thankfully never said anything. Years later, I found out she had asked Aunty to look after me if anything happened to her.

As if things couldn't get any worse, we moved. Our new place was a little cedar-shingled shack on the other side of town. It was cold and damp and looked as destitute as I felt. It had two small bedrooms, a dingy living room that barely brought in any light, and a big kitchen with peeling linoleum. There was a big back-yard with a walk-in chicken coop that I turned into a fort. I spent most of my time there, reading or daydreaming of the day I would find my father and he would take me to live with him.

The first few months weren't too bad, but then Don started to criticize Mom more and more. Either she was lazy or she defended me too much. Sometimes I heard him hitting her in the bedroom and she would cry and plead for him to stop, but he wouldn't. How I hated him and wished him dead! Every time he struck her, I felt as if he were hitting me. All I could do was bury my face in my pillow and silently scream, "Die! Die! Die!"

Mom started drinking again, and to my surprise, Don bought her whisky or beer even though he continued going to AA and accepting his yearly "birthday cakes" for staying sober. Mom was so skinny and sickly looking, I thought for sure she was going to die, which sent me into a panic as Don would then be my sole guardian. She was covered in red blotches and could barely walk without help. I have destroyed all of the pictures from that time, as they filled me with such hatred and disgust. In them, Mom looked nothing like herself, more like a concentration camp survivor.

Don felt we needed family counselling and so he arranged for us to see a psychiatrist. The psychiatrist talked to Mom and Don first and then he saw me. I tried to tell him what was happening but he would only say, "Now, Greg, you know that's not true. Don loves you and only wants the very best for you. Maybe *you* should try a bit harder." Try harder! I was so petrified of Don I wouldn't dare speak without his permission. Mom was so whacked out on booze and pills, she sat around in a daze, oblivious to everything.

Three months after our counselling began, Don and the psychiatrist decided I should go into foster care. By now, Mom was so sick and detached, I could have been sent to China and she wouldn't have noticed. I didn't even see Aunty any more as Don had changed his work schedule to be home by the time school let out. I did my chores and homework, did the supper dishes and went to bed. I wasn't allowed to "bother" Mom, who seldom ever came out of the bedroom.

One morning, before school, a social worker came to the house. She talked to Don for quite a while and then she helped me pack. I refused to let Don see me cry and did as the worker told me. Before I knew it, I was sitting in her car and tears were running down my face. I hadn't even been allowed to say good-bye to Mom. As we were pulling out of the driveway, I caught myself silently praying, *Please, Creator, look after Mom for me.*

She made an occupation out of keeping other
Women's children   flawless   Even bone china
Looked cheap up against that keemooch smile

Those social workers had some nerve making
Her a saint   Mother Teresa would have spit
If she knew about that cashy advance   Taking

Me in   What did I know about Christian duty
I was a wild Indian fresh from the slums
Defacing her neighbourhood   making a tipi

Out back   I had this thing for authenticity
Westerns were my favorite   I wanted a mini
Village   to be the chief   not her idea of

Civilization   tho a haircut made me look
Tame
She couldn't break me like her other kids

Milly Spencer was the strictest woman I had ever met. She was in her fifties, tall and thin with greying hair pinned into a beehive, long and sharp features, and steel-blue eyes which looked as if they could catch even God doing something wrong. Her lips were thin and pursed and she seldom smiled. "Hello and welcome to my home," she said flatly in an English accent. She took my suitcase from the worker, said goodbye, and then ushered me into the house as if I was a criminal.

The Spencers's large, beautiful home on River Road in the expensive part of town, overlooking the Fraser River, was filled with antiques, china, and Persian rugs. Red velvet drapes hung from the windows and there was a crystal chandelier in the dining room. On the main floor was a large kitchen and pantry, the dining room and living room, washroom, the Spencers's bedroom, a guest room, and my room. Downstairs were the bedrooms of the other foster kids and their daughter, all of whom were older than I was, the laundry room, another wash-room, and the rec-room. I was overwhelmed by the luxury.

It was obvious the Spencers had money, and I couldn't figure out why they would be taking in foster kids. But I soon realized the reason once Mrs. Spencer told me the rules of the house. "It's my understanding," she began, "you're used to running wild. There'll be none of that around here. This is a God-fearing home and I will not stand for any monkey business. You are not allowed to use foul language or take the Lord's name in vain. You are also expected to do the dishes and take out the garbage like everyone else. I will be checking your room regularly, and if it's messy, you'll be punished. And once again," she stressed. "You are not to go into any of the bedrooms or *touch anything*!"

Mrs. Spencer was married to a fisherman whom everyone called Red. He was seldom ever home, and when he was, Mrs. Spencer treated him much the same way she treated us kids. They had a teenage daughter who made it clear she didn't approve of her mother's godly mission to save the more unfortunate. Besides me, there were three other foster kids: two eighteen-year-old boys and a sixteen-year-old-girl who spent a great deal of time alone in her room.

I knew loneliness only too well. I lay awake that night and listened to the train whistle in the distance. One day, I, too, would leave this horrible town. But first I would kill Don and rescue Mom. Aunty would come with us, and together we would find happiness again. But night after night, my dreams began to fade and I found myself moving through each day like a robot, ever hopeful that Mom was still alive.

Mrs. Spencer loved to go to the beauty parlour, and faithfully every week after school she took me with her. Having to go with her seemed punishment enough, but having to listen to those old hens banter back and forth was pure torture. I recall one afternoon as I sat waiting for Mrs. Spencer. As usual, she was complaining about Red being gone and how hard it was to manage us kids alone. She suddenly grew quiet, but then I overheard her talking about Mom. "It's an absolute disgrace," she ranted. "How a mother could dress her child in rags." The hairdresser turned to look at me, and I felt so ashamed I wanted to crawl under my seat. But then I felt angry. Mom had always done her best to keep me in nice clothes. Besides, Mrs. Spencer received money from social services to buy me new ones. The entire year in her care, I got a pair of runners, some underwear, and socks.

The one good thing about living with the Spencers was that I was away from Don. Although Mrs. Spencer was strict, she was fair, sometimes more than others. She allowed me to bring home Indian books and even allowed me to watch westerns on TV, although it was obvious she didn't agree with the Indian way of life, often telling me about Jesus and the Bible. She never once hit or humiliated me. As long as I did my chores, kept my room neat and tidy, and asked permission to do things, she was agreeable, even kind. Still, she made it clear I was a ward of the province and I should be grateful, as she'd done Mom a great favour by taking me in. "After all," she always reminded me, "you could have ended up in an orphanage."

Already eight months had gone by and I hadn't heard from Mom; I was convinced she was either in the hospital or dead. Then one evening after supper the phone rang. I was in the pantry putting some fruit jars away and Mrs. Spencer was in the kitchen. "How many times have I told you not to call here," she said, talking barely above a whisper. "Do you want to lose him for good!" She hung up the phone and went back to putting the leftovers away. I came into the kitchen, and trying not to sound hopeful, asked her who had called. "Never mind!" she snapped. "Go to your room!"

I threw myself on the bed feeling many different emotions. I wanted to see Mom more than anything. And yet I was just happy to know she was still alive, even though I couldn't be with her. I thought about Mom and how our lives had been stolen from us by complete strangers. I decided if I couldn't see or talk to her, then I'd talk to her with my heart. I would send her all of my bad feelings, and she in turn would send back feelings of love and hope. At last, we had something that no one could take away! But I also felt overwhelming anger, a new rebelliousness.

Later I would learn that Mom had left Don and was in a transition house for battered women. She told me that he had threatened to kill her if she left him, and that he blamed me for everything. He also promised to do everything in his power to have me taken away permanently. But the RCMP stepped in, and he was given a restraining order.

When Mom finally left Don, she weighed less than a hundred pounds and was covered from head to toe in bruises. When her health did not improve, the doctors did numerous tests and finally discovered she had lupus. They put her on all sorts of medication, and for the first time in years, her health improved. She was then thirty-two, the same age I am now.

Nine

House of Rooms

Two days after Mom called the Spencers, I ran away. I decided no one was going to keep me from seeing her, and one afternoon, instead of going home, I went to Grandma's. To my disappointment, Mom wasn't there (she was in the transition house) and Grandma called Mrs. Spencer. When I got hysterical and refused to go back, Grandma said it would only make things harder on Mom. Mrs. Spencer came to get me and she seemed concerned and understanding. But once we were in the car, she fixed me with her icy stare and told me that I was grounded for a month. She sent me to my room and I recall feeling almost happy I'd caused her trouble.

Two months later, after the school year finished, I was placed back with Mom. I wasn't sorry to leave Mrs. Spencer — she could never love me. We moved into an apartment and tried our best to start over. But we were like two strangers trying to find a home in one another, each of us displaced in our own way. The past year showed on Mom's face. She looked old and haggard, and her eyes were dull and lifeless. It was as if Don had completely killed her spirit. And yet, like the picture of the Iron Soldier that Mom had bought after we returned to Maple Ridge from Washington, we silently watched the days slip by, neither one of us talking about the past, forever hopeful our lives would once again be safe and happy.

While I was in care, Aunty had reunited with Chuck, her common-law husband, and they'd moved into a little house closer to the river. I stayed with her as often as I could, and she continued to teach me about the old ways. I had practically forgotten the Cree she'd taught me, and faithfully practised the words she wrote down. As I recited them for her she would laugh at my poor pronunciation and say, *"Ma! moon-e-yas ke-pe-kisk-we-win"* (You speak like a white person). She continued to tell me stories, first in Cree and then in English, and over time my pronunciation improved. But still I was easily frustrated, feeling as if my tongue had been cut out. *"Tapway* (for sure), my boy,"* she'd encourage. "Don't you worry. Aunty will make you a good Cree speaker yet."

Although Aunty had grown up in a convent school, she managed to retain a lot of the traditions her mother had taught her. She taught me the importance of honesty and respect, often reminding me that everything we did or said was considered *medicine*, and that we needed to be aware of our actions. *"Peyah-tik"* (walk softly, give something great thought), she would always remind me, especially when I became angry.

Aunty was a firm believer in omens and signs. She told me how the old people considered owls to be messengers of death. In fact, she said, when her first two babies died in nothern Alberta, three owls had sat on her clothesline outside, hooting long into the night, for almost a week. She also told me that if a bird flies in your house, someone will take sick or die. Besides these grim prophesies, Aunty explained to me the importance of dreams. They were the Creator's way of talking to you, of telling you something sacred. But there were also dreams that signified good or bad luck. For example, if you dreamed of a baby peeing on you, it was good luck. And, if you dreamed of a loose tooth or losing your teeth, a relative was sure to die.

Besides the *We-sak-e-jack* stories, my other favourite story was about the Wild Fairy who lived in the forest and flew above the treetops late at night, looking down upon the sleeping world. She had long hair down to her feet and wore a necklace of different-coloured ribbons, all of which had great power and magic. If someone was lucky enough to see her, even in dreams, she bestowed upon them one wish. Night after night, I remember hoping to dream of her, knowing full well what I would do with my wish. I would make Don disappear for good.

Grade seven seemed like such a big step. Next year I would be a teenager, starting high school. That seemed weird enough, but the first day of school was even stranger. For the first time, I had a crush on someone — my teacher. Mr. Barnes was the most handsome man I'd ever seen. He was six feet tall with wavy brown hair and big blue eyes. He was athletic, young, and he smiled and winked, which made everyone in class, especially the girls, giggle and blush. My insides felt like jelly by the time I got home. I would have Mr. Barnes for the whole year, and I had already decided I wanted him to marry Mom. Everything would be good then. Mom would be happy and I would have a dad — only it didn't feel quite right. I wasn't sure how boys were supposed to feel about their dads. I certainly hadn't felt this way towards Tommy, Uncle Tim or Don. But now I loved Mr. Barnes and couldn't wait to see him every day.

Halfway through the school year there was a parent-teacher meeting. At last, Mom was going to meet Mr. Barnes (I had talked about him endlessly) and I was sure she would love him just as much as I did. My marks were all good and I was quiet and well behaved, even good at sports now — a perfect son. Mr. Barnes liked me and now all Mom had to do was invite him for supper (I had dropped numerous hints). But she only talked to him briefly, said goodbye, and then we left. She hadn't even shaken his hand. I was heart-broken. How could she be so blind! If she could marry someone like Don, then why not Mr. Barnes?

In spite of my broken dream, I continued to do well in school.

My love of books grew to be an obsession and I read everything from the Hardy Boys/Nancy Drew mysteries to the Louis L'Amour westerns. Once a week, Mom and I went to Mrs. Merc's bookstore and I would find something on Indians. I still didn't know if I was really an Indian, but inside I felt like one. When I asked Mom she shrugged her shoulders, adding that my father might have had Indian blood. She seemed indifferent, and once again I thought it best not to bring up Aunty's comments. Still, Mom was supportive of my interest and encouraged me to read books about Indians. I got a copy of Dee Brown's *Bury My Heart at Wounded Knee* and pored over it, mortified by the atrocities done to American Indian people. My romantic ideas of living in a tipi and galloping across the plains in a feathered warbonnet were soon replaced by anger — the same anger that sometimes skated around the edges of Aunty's voice when she talked about white people.

It seems astounding to me now that Mom was so oblivious to her *own* Indianness, projecting it on to my father, whom she knew so little about. I knew race didn't matter to her. She was one of the most non-racist people I have ever known. Still, I find it odd that she, like Aunty Sandra, would never have questioned her ethnicity. After all, Grandpa looked Native. But then again, my grandmother never recognized it, at least not in words, as they were growing up.

Around this time, Alex Haley's book *Roots* was made into a TV miniseries. In spite of the subject matter, Mom let me watch it. How similar it was to Dee Brown's book and how angry it made me feel! Mom explained it was good to be angry, to understand the injustices done to people of colour, but to also remember that out of any struggle came determination and freedom. I would think of her words many years later, reading a letter that she'd written to the local paper during the Oka crisis, her own Indianness having ironically come full circle.

I felt as if I had entered a new room in my body, a room filled with new ideas and emotions. I had so many questions and so few answers. Why had the Indians been killed and put on to reservations? Why had the black people been enslaved and treated like animals? Even more confusing, why did I cry for Mr. Barnes and why did I sometimes imagine him without clothes? Why wasn't I like the other boys at school? Why didn't I have a dad? Why did I feel so alone in the world?

I began to feel as if I was floating out of my body, floating above the heads of my classmates, above Mom and Grandma, even Aunty. I felt rootless and distant, like a ghost moving from room to room, never quite settling in one place. My muscles and joints began to ache and I felt as if invisible hands were pulling my arms and legs. Sometimes, too, I had sexual thoughts about other boys. I knew it wasn't normal, and I began to think something was horribly wrong with me.

Then, my worst fears came true. A month before school ended, Mom started to see Don again. How could she, after everything he had done to us? But she swore up and down he had changed, which I knew he hadn't. I could see it in his eyes, I could hear it in his voice. He was like a deadly snake who had slithered back into our lives, just waiting and looking for the perfect opportunity to strike.

I was so terrified Mom would get back with him, I couldn't sleep for weeks. When I did sleep, my dreams were always the same. I was alone in an old abandoned house with no electricity. Everything was black and I crawled from room to room, desperately looking for a safe place to hide. I hid in closets and cupboards, careful not to make any noise or breathe too loud. But still I could hear Don's footsteps coming closer. Thankfully, I always woke before he found me, but the fear stayed with me like a rock in my stomach. I carried it throughout the day, awoke with it at night, forever aware of its presence.

By now Don was practically living with us again, and it seemed as if Mom had never left him. Of course, he was nice to me in front of her, but as soon as her back was turned, he shot me deadly looks. Once again I ran to Aunty, but she was powerless to do anything. I felt as if I was stuck in quicksand and slowly sinking while everyone stood by helplessly watching. Mom appeared oblivious to everything.

Summer came, and with it my thirteenth birthday. I was now officially a teenager, which meant more freedom but also a new set of rules. I had made some friends at school and spent the summer with them, drinking and experimenting with drugs. Some of them had girlfriends and bragged about the sexy things they did. I wanted to brag, too. But more than anything I wanted to belong. I pushed the thoughts of boys out of my head and started to look at girls the way I was supposed to. For the first time in my life, I felt a part of something. I felt like a real teenager, and more important, normal.

Towards the end of summer, Mom and Don sat me down and told me that once again we were moving. Don gave me one of his looks and I felt the rock in my stomach burst into a million pieces.

The next few weeks were like a landslide, everything happening so quickly. Mom began to pack the apartment, throwing our lives into boxes as if we were going on a splendid holiday. I begged her to reconsider, but she wouldn't listen. What had Don done to make her go back? What had he said? And what about me? Suddenly the memories of the past came flooding back: the countless times she'd left me, how I never knew from one minute to the next where I'd be, how it was all *her* fault — everything! I began to hate her more and more every day. She didn't love me.

The past, Tommy and Leah, Washington, Abby and the old ugly building, Don and Mrs. Spencer — none of it seemed real. Even Mom was an aberration, a character in my distorted life. Only *I* was *real,* with the rage silently growing inside me.

Like the abandoned house in my nightmares, I crawled into a

room so deep within myself, no one would ever find me. There, I could imagine a life filled with happiness and love. Don could beat me until I was black and blue, but he couldn't hurt me. Mom could float off in her own dreams, too, weightless and happy. I had myself and nothing else mattered — I no longer needed anyone.

Ten

Roots in a Dry Desert

Ladybug, Ladybug, fly away home. Your house is on fire and your children all gone, all except one and that's for Ann, for she's crept under the frying pan. The silly rhyme rang over and over in my head like the church bells on Christmas Eve. No matter how hard I tried, I couldn't get it out of my head. It was as if I was being warned of something. What I didn't know. But the rhyme stuck with me long after we moved.

Our new home was surprisingly the nicest place we ever lived. It was a two-storey town house in Coquitlam, which was almost ten miles from Maple Ridge. Upstairs were three bedrooms and a washroom and downstairs there was a large bright living room, separate dining room, kitchen and sitting area, another washroom, and plenty of storage space. With floor-to-ceiling windows, the entire place reminded me of a solarium. It seemed like a new beginning.

Mom, Don, and I got settled just before school started. My new school, my fifth one, was two miles away, and I was apprehensive about going. It was huge and relatively new, housing students from grades eight to twelve in a maze of offices and classrooms. Unlike the other eighth graders, I found it hard to make friends. Once again, I didn't fit in. At first, I was quiet and inconspicuous, content to be in my own enclosed world.

I needed to be somebody. It didn't take me long to figure out who was cool and who wasn't. I wasn't a jock and I most definitely didn't want to be seen as a geek, so I became a "rocker." I begged Mom to buy me a black leather jacket, and to my amazement, Don got me one. I grew my hair long and started to dress like the lead singers of Judas Priest and AC/DC, with whom I became totally obsessed, loving their screaming guitars, wild drum solos, and harsh lyrics. More than anything, I related to the black message behind their music. It was loud and in-your-face — everything I wanted to be!

Now I liked being thought of as rebellious. I made friends with other kids like me: kids who came from-fucked up homes or homes where their parents didn't give a damn about them. Sometimes we skipped school and hung out at the park, drinking and smoking pot. I was careful to hide it from Mom and Don, cautious not to skip too many days or come home too wasted.

Surprisingly, I did well on my first report card, getting mostly Bs and Cs, all except for math and science, which I found boring and useless. I didn't care about algebra or root squares — I certainly would never be rich or designing any buildings. As far as science went, the only subject I found interesting was biology. The human body was on my mind a lot. Girls, too, were supposed to be on my mind. But like a thief, I found myself stealing glances at the boys in gym class. By now I was sure something was wrong with me. Was I a fag like some of the boys who got beaten up after school? But I just couldn't be! I wasn't a sissy or a geek. I was too cool. Besides, I had plenty of girls who wanted to date me.

Around this time I made friends with the only other Indian in school. Now, I was certain that I was an Indian, more conscious of the way people looked at me, hearing comments in the hallway like "wagon-burner" or "chug," sometimes even "fag." Emma was a year older than I was and she lived in a foster home. Like

Abby, she was tough-looking and had an attitude to match. She came to school whenever she wanted, and because she had a bad reputation, no one dared mess with her. The school year wasn't even half over and she'd already beaten up four people — three of them guys. At first Emma thought I was a goof and wouldn't have anything to do with me. But then one weekend at a party we both got drunk and told each other about our lives. I talked about Aunty and the things she'd taught me. She said that I was lucky because she hadn't seen her parents in over ten years. I also told her about Don and the horrible things he'd done to Mom and me. She told me that her dad had beaten her, too, and that's why she'd been taken away by social services.

After that, Emma and I stuck together like glue. Everyone called us names, but Emma always set them straight. Even my own friends started to call me "chief" and teased me about my "tough squaw." Although their comments hurt and filled me with shame, I laughed along with them, feeling guilty for betraying Emma, secretly hoping that the novelty of our friendship would soon get stale, which, of course, it didn't. Suddenly I was more of an outcast than I wanted to be. I began to dread going to school and felt completely alone, especially if Emma wasn't there.

We started to learn about Canadian history in social studies. The teacher read from textbooks and talked about Indians as if they were all dead or living in a mysterious cave somewhere in the Grand Canyon. By the time we got to the settling of the West and the Northwest Rebellion, I was humiliated. How could Aunty possibly say we were half-breeds? Louis Riel was crazy and a traitor to the Canadian government. The Métis weren't Indians at all, but Frenchmen pretending to be Indians. They had no culture or language and nothing to be proud of. At least the Indians, no matter how ragged and poor, had an interesting culture. They had beautiful costumes and danced and sang. They spoke different languages — like Aunty and me —

and had medicines and secret knowledge about the spirit world.

I decided Aunty must be wrong about us being half-breeds. We were *Nay-he-yow-wuk* — Crees! After all, we spoke Cree, did beadwork, and used Indian medicines. I still questioned if Mom was Native, thinking more about my dad and what she'd said about his possibly having Indian blood. Finally, I asked Grandma about my dad, and, to my surprise, she told me that he was Italian. In spite of my disappointment, I felt that I had at least been given a place to start. I caught the bus into Vancouver on the weekends and hung around the Italian neighbourhood, hoping by some miracle that I would run into him. But after about a month of this, I realized I didn't look Italian at all. I checked with Grandma again, but she denied ever telling me that, saying instead that my dad was English. By now I was so confused I gave up ever finding him. I knew he was out there somewhere, but chances were I would never find him or know anything about him.

My only clue to my identity was the mirror and books. If I wasn't Italian or English (I ruled that out because I certainly didn't resemble the Queen or Prince Charles), then I must be Native. But a different kind of Indian — a white Indian like Dustin Hoffman in *Little Big Man*. Either way it was settled, and no one, not Mom or Don or Grandma, could stop me from finding my tribe.

Oddly enough, Don relaxed with the whole Indian idea, and to my surprise he let me have Indian books in the house. I couldn't figure out his change of heart, but I certainly wasn't going to question it, as he now allowed me to see Aunty again. When I spent the weekends with her, as always, I savoured her stories and the things she taught me. One story was of great interest to me because it involved *sah-ke-ye-towin muskeeg-ke* (love medicine), which was very powerful and few people knew about. It concerned an older woman named *Ooh-hoo-koot* (Owl-nose), who used love medicine on a young man with whom she was smitten, but who was ignoring her.

Ooh-hoo-koot's medicine was strong, for she had gone to see a well-known medicine man whose expertise in matters of love was renowned throughout the country. Sure enough, the young man fell deeply in love with her. They were married and moved up north, far away from family and friends. But over the years *Ooh-hoo-koot* grew bored of her husband's childlike ways and she became restless to find a man she could feel equal to. She began to stay away for days at a time, and it was rumoured that she'd taken another lover.

But the young man was so in love with her, he refused to believe it. Then one night there was a knock upon the door. "Forgive me," said a strange man, "but there has been a terrible accident. I am sorry to tell you your wife is dead."

"Ha!" laughed the young man. "You must be mistaken. My wife is visiting her family."

"Perhaps," replied the stranger, "it is you who are mistaken. She has been with her lover only a few miles from here. Last night his house caught fire, and both of them are dead."

But as the weeks turned into months the young man still did not believe the story. He went out of his mind, searching the towns and woods. He kept vigil at the window each and every night. He even went back to their old home, looking for her. But no one had seen or heard from her.

And so, over the years, the young man grew sicker and sicker. Finally, when he was on his deathbed, a medicine man was summoned. First the old man shook his rattle over him and then he placed two small white stones on his eyes. Sure enough, the stones turned black, and the old man exclaimed, "Haw! I have found the sickness. It is love sickness." But it was too late. The young man died that night. "This is a terrible thing," said the old man. "The medicine is far too strong. *Ooh-hoo-koot much-chee-manitow* (Owl-nose is the devil)! She is greedy even from the world beyond."

Aunty seldom told me about these kinds of medicines, saying that I didn't need to know about them, as they were very powerful and dangerous. She always warned me not to leave strands of my hair or any of my personal belongings behind, because someone could put medicine on me. As I grew older and more concerned about love, more so infatuation, I often thought about *Ooh-hoo-koot*, secretly wishing that I had some of her medicine, although the mere thought of it made me shudder.

Aunty continued to tell me various stories about her childhood in northern Alberta, mostly about her days at the convent school and her friend Agnes, with whom she was forever getting into trouble. She told me about the time she and Agnes had to clean the chapel. They got into the communion wine and started to laugh and sing, "I don't care what dey say, all da *moon-e-yas iskway-suk* (white girls) *ke-ta-say* (take down their pants)." Sister Dennis came charging in and they were hauled into Mother Superior's office. Aunty said they were given extra work and had to say their rosary, but it was worth getting drunk on "Christ's blood."

Thinking back to Aunty's stories, to many of my childhood experiences with her, I realize now how much humour I had grown up with, how Aunty had always used jokes and teasing to lessen the hardships of life. For Native people, humour has always been an important part of our culture, a way to see our own idiosyncrasies and the foolishness of others. It is inherent in our stories and legends, entwined in the very fabric of our lives and traditions. The old people love to tease and laugh, poking fun at one another in a serious world.

I realize there is very little humour in my own story. I wish that there was more. But my childhood holds few things to laugh at. It took me a long time to develop a sense of humour, to see the world as a funny, mixed-up place, a place we all have to exist in.

That summer, in spite of Aunty's surprising disapproval, I started going to powwows. It was as if I'd finally found my rightful place. I was so hypnotized by the dancers, swirling and swaying in their colourful outfits, all moving in unison to the steady beat of the drums. I worked laboriously to get an outfit together, determined to be a world champion powwow dancer. Grandma sewed me a ribbon shirt, satin-fringed apron, yoke, and cuffs. Even Mom gave me money to buy beads and feathers. And Don didn't say anything.

Yet I was still afraid to wear my outfit or dance in public. I didn't look right — I was too white. People gave me strange looks. I felt unsure if I was even an Indian at all. How I would have given anything to have black hair and brown eyes!

Then towards the end of the summer, I came across a poster advertising a powwow at Peace Arch Park, which was near the Canada/U.S. border. It was only two hours away, and I begged Mom and Don to take me, promising never to ask for anything else. Once again, to my surprise, Don agreed, and the following weekend I packed up my outfit and we headed off. Mom and Don dropped me off, saying they would be back in a couple of hours.

To my disappointment, the powwow was small. There were only a few dancers and one drum group. I took a seat and watched some of the younger dancers straggle by, wishing that I had the nerve to join them. My toes were tapping to the drum, and before I knew it, I was in the dance circle — only I was dancing the wrong way. An elder in a wheelchair gestured me over. She looked to be in her early seventies. Her hair was still dark and neatly braided, decorated with beautifully beaded hairties that matched her buckskin dress and leggings. She wore eagle plumes in her hair and on her fingers were various turquoise rings. "I've been watching you dance," she began, "and you're a very good dancer. But we always dance in a circle, the way the sun goes. Do you have an outfit?"

"Yes," I said, feeling embarrassed, suddenly wishing that I hadn't come.

"Oh, that's good then," she smiled. "Did your parents bring it?"

"They're shopping," I confessed, feeling even more embarrassed.

"That's okay. Did you bring it with you?"

"Yes," I nodded.

"Well, then," she said, "it would make me very happy to see you dancing in it." She directed me to the change room and I hurriedly slipped into my outfit. How proud I felt! I danced as hard as I could, displaying my fancy footwork, especially for the old lady.

Afterwards, she called me over and there were tears in her eyes. She asked me what tribe I came from and I told her that I wasn't sure, although I thought Cree. She said that it didn't matter because she wanted to adopt me, and said for me to call her Grandma. Mom and Don came to get me, and before we left, I introduced Mom to Grandma Francis. Grandma gave me her phone number, kissed me goodbye, and made me promise to practise my dancing every day.

Little did I know who had adopted me. Dorothy Francis was a highly respected elder from the Waywayseecappo Band in Manitoba, who had devoted her life to promoting and preserving Native culture. In 1964, she was awarded the Gold Key Award by *Chatelaine* magazine for services to her people. She had worked with the CBC on an Indian program called "North Country Fair," acting as hostess, speaking Saulteaux and English on the air. She had also worked as a family counsellor, had set up the first Winnipeg Powwow Club, and had even dined with the Queen. Dorothy was an inspiration to Native people across the country.

Despite the questions I had about my father, my life now was relatively happy. In spite of the racial and gay comments, I had done well in school, even managed to pass math and science, if only barely. I was able to keep a few friends, although I no longer saw Emma, as she'd moved to a different foster home. I missed her a great deal and wished, for purely selfish reasons, that she was still there. I hated being the only Indian in school — invisible or not.

By the beginning of grade nine, everything started to go wrong again. I should have known that Don's old personality would return. Mom and Don weren't getting along, and he seemed to be on her case about everything, primarily me. He said that I was too carried away with the Indian stuff, that I had neglected everything else in my life. He took my outfit away and refused to give it back unless I started to get As and Bs on my report card. Furthermore, I wasn't allowed to talk to Aunty or Grandma Francis. I needed to stop acting like a "God damn reserve Indian" and I should start applying myself to more important things like school and getting a job.

Don had served in the Korean War and he believed that discipline made the weak, as he often called me, strong. Thus began my regimented life of routine. In the mornings he would burst into my room, shake my bed, and stand over me, screaming the day's orders. Like Mom, I wasn't a morning person and found it extremely difficult to organize my thoughts upon command. Of course, I would forget half of the things I was supposed to do and Don would get after me, always telling Mom what a lazy, useless piece of shit I was. I went to school irate and distracted, just itching for a fight with anyone — even the teachers. Most days, I skipped school and went to the mall or library until it was time to go home.

Steadily things got worse — to the point where Don was hitting Mom again. Only it wasn't like before. He was like an insane sergeant, forcing her to her knees, slapping her over and over if she didn't bark back his orders. Mom suffered in silence, once again recoiling to the bedroom, over-medicating herself to numb the pain. By now she and Don had separate bedrooms and barely spoke at all. It was like living under the constant threat of a time-bomb.

I was determined to kill him. Obsessed with the idea, I lay awake at night, visualizing and plotting his death. I imagined slitting his throat or plunging a knife into his back. Because of my age, or so I believed, the police couldn't do anything, nor all the courts or magistrates in the world. They would understand. They had to! Don deserved to die. And in the most painful way possible.

Eleven

The Long Road Ahead

Now that I am a grown man, it's hard to imagine how Don once instilled such fear and hatred in me. Upon writing this part of the story, I have found myself digging through Mom's old things: letters and legal papers, cards and newspaper clippings, her moving poetry that I am sure she once dreamed of publishing, poems of my teenage angst, mementos from a long-ago time, and, of course, hundreds of pictures, many of which are of Don.

Looking at him now, after all these years, I see for the first time that he was just a plain and ordinary man, neither handsome nor ugly: a man with a flat chest and skinny arms, a thinning crown of black hair neatly greased and combed to the side; a forced smile behind which emanates the unspoken tortures of his own childhood. How small and weak he seems now! I could almost forgive him, even let go of the past, but the hate I carry has been with me for so long, I can't imagine it ever leaving me.

I have thought about Don a great deal over the years, particularly about the self-hate he carried for being Native, the same self-hate I carried for being Métis and gay. Years after Mom finally left him, she told me that his mother was a hereditary chief from northern B.C., that he, too, could have been a chief, but that he had disowned his mother and her family. His father was Scottish, and for some reason had left his mother when Don was still a boy. Yet, Don refused to acknowledge his mother and idealized his father. Ironically, his history was much like my grandfather's. One man chose a life of brutality, the other of kindness.

Around this time I befriended twin brothers named Toby and Terrance who were the same age as I was and lived down the street in another townhouse complex. Their parents were Dutch and had come to Canada before the twins were born. They were born-again Christians and were loving and kind, forever support-ive of their sons. I thought of them as the perfect family and wanted more than anything to live with them.

The twins were unlike my other friends. They were thought-ful and kind, never mean or judgemental. They didn't skip school, drink, or do drugs. Instead they played sports and went to church with their parents. When I told them about Don and the horrible situation Mom and I were in, they listened sympa-thetically, shaking their heads in disbelief. I am sure they told their parents, for a short time later I was being invited over for dinner and to spend the night.

Not long after I met the twins, I befriended another classmate who also lived in our complex. Like me, Sean had a stepfather who was just as terrible as Don. His mother was quiet and timid, with the same hollow eyes as Mom. Sean and I became best friends, and we often skipped school together. Unlike the twins, we could relate on a different level; both of us hated our stepfa-thers and the control they had over our lives. There was also something else we had in common — and I didn't like it.

Sean was forever being singled out at school for being gay. He wore his persecution silently, seldom sticking up for himself. I remember thinking that people teased him because he was soft-spoken and somewhat effeminate. I knew that I, too, had those qualities, but I did my best to hide them. Also I had learned (thanks to Emma) to fight back no matter what the cost. Somehow the idea of suffering in silence instilled more shame in me than if I got a good licking.

Nevertheless, Sean and I remained friends. It wasn't long before we were being called "bum-buddies." Luckily, most times I walloped the other guy (often thinking about Don), winning on pure adrenaline alone.

I hurt when I think about those times, about Sean. So many gay men, like so many Native people and people of colour, are at the complete mercy of a society that condones homophobia and racism, and so many of us go through life silently accepting those sterotypes, ultimately dying spiritless and shame-ridden.

There is an experience I had with Sean and the twins, an experience that most, if not all, young people have. I share it in the context of my own adolescent growth, the fear and denial I carried because of it, in the hope of deconstructing what should be a very normal experience for gay/lesbian/bisexual youth who are struggling with sexual identity issues, issues that are neither accepted nor addressed in high schools across this country.

Because Sean and I were friends, the twins also befriended him. One weekend, Sean and I came to spend the night, and as usual there was plenty of sexual innuendo and playful jousting. Although I had never had sex, I knew enough about it from reading books and watching R-rated movies. I had even seen a few movies with gay characters, although it seemed odd to see them actually kiss. Nevertheless, come bedtime, we all ambled up to the loft where the twins slept. Toby suggested that we mutually masturbate. Sean, being normally shy and unsure of himself, looked over at me, as if the suggestion was some sort of trap. But I was just as surprised. At first, Terrance disputed the whole idea, but his brother was insistent. So there we were, four four-teen-year-old boys, naked as the day we were born. And how beautiful the twins were! With each stroke of their hands, their bodies seemed to lift into flight, catching the light of the table lamp, accentuating their every muscle and movement. I was so awe-struck by their developed bodies — mine had yet to change — their shyness and hunger, I couldn't even touch myself. Of course, much later the entire scene would become the basis of innumerable fantasies — fantasies that I felt were wrong!

A short time later, the twins gave themselves over to God completely. They tried their best to save me, practically begging me to forgive them for their shameful act. I went to church with them a few times, but the spirit they had found certainly didn't come knocking upon my door. Gradually we lost touch, although I saw them at school every day.

As for Sean, we, too, drifted apart. He continued to get harassed and beaten up, forever wearing his shame and helplessness like a heavy yoke around his neck. I ran into him years later in the gay district in Vancouver. Like me, he had changed and grown up. We each carried our own scars, some of them the same, others different. I recall the look of happiness and sadness that came across his face when I mentioned the twins. I watched him cross the street with his boyfriend, his head down as it had always been. Two years later, I was flipping through a gay newspaper and came across his obituary and picture. He had died of an AIDS-related illness at twenty-one. I wanted to cry but I couldn't. I felt he didn't need my tears, but something more constructive — like my own self-acceptance — something that would take me another ten years to find.

By now, Mom was a complete zombie, holed up in her room, flying high on pills, flying to what I assumed was a much better place. Sometimes I crept into her room and took a few of her valium or sleeping pills. They worked like magic. I could sleep and sleep and sleep. My dreams were filled with vivid colours, open fields and crystalline lakes. The sun never went down.

In reality, I fell so behind in my studies, there was absolutely no catching up. By mid-semester my grades were so poor, I felt there was no point in continuing with school. I had flunked everything except for English, which somehow came easily to me.

I came home one afternoon, and as soon as I stepped through the front door, I heard Don beating up Mom. The pent-up emotions, the fear and hate, the immense loathing I had for him, came flooding out like a bursting dam. I recall vividly the sound of Mom's pathetic cries and pleading, the sound of Don's hand as he struck her. The first thing I noticed was the cloth wall-hanging with the embroidered words of the "Serenity Prayer" that Don's daughter Sherry had given to him one Christmas. I grabbed it off the wall and tore it into pieces. As if pushed by an invisible force, I bolted up the stairs and kicked open the bedroom door. Mom was on her knees and Don stood over her, yelling and hitting her.

"You son of a bitch! I am going to kill you! Get your fucking hands off her!" Determined, I felt strong and self-assured. Don came lunging towards me and I took off down the hallway. Just as I got to my room, he caught hold of the back of my neck and started to choke me. Mom was at the door, screaming, but he was like a wounded animal. I somehow managed to wrestle out of his hold, and kneed him in the groin. He buckled over and fell to his knees, holding himself and groaning. I can never describe the sheer power I felt — the victory! I looked down at him and spat, "Don't you dare touch us again, you fucking bastard!"

After that I felt invincible, unbreakable, as if nothing could ever hurt me again. Unbeknownst to Mom and Don, I dropped out of school. As before, I hung out in the library, taking solitude in my only escape — Mom's pills and books. My life was a blur of pictures and words, places that I dreamed of going, places that only existed in the pages of travel books. With each pill, reality slipped away, taking everyone — Aunty, Grandma, Mom and Don, Grandma Francis, my friends — with it.

I look back now, grateful that I never discovered heroin. The years that I spent working with street kids have given me a feeling of grace and gratitude. Heroin is the ultimate escape, the ultimate state of peace and reality where nothing else matters, except the next fix. It's hard to imagine Mom strung out on that stuff as a young woman, selling herself to strangers, wanting so desperately to escape whatever it was that first led her to stick a needle in her arm. In spite of my own past addictions, I consider myself lucky to be alive — if luck has anything to do with it. Unlike Mom, who spent a lifetime dependent upon drugs and alcohol, unlike a lot of the street kids who died of overdoses or violence — thanks to the Creator, I survived.

In spite of the beatings, Mom's health was relatively good, as the lupus was in remission. But then she took deathly sick with double pneumonia. Don rushed her to the hospital, but her lungs were so weak, the doctors were sure she would die. No matter what they did, her lungs just kept filling up with fluid. She wavered between life and death for weeks. The family was called in and plans were made for her funeral. I was in a numbing state of shock, feeling completely disconnected to anything real.

Amidst the worry and confusion, no one considered my future. I certainly couldn't live with Grandma, nor had my aunts or Aunty Georgina volunteered to take me, which meant that Don would now be my guardian. I was panic-stricken, determined with every fibre of my being that Mom just had to get better! I remember Don taking me into the washroom at Grandma's, and for the first time ever he broke down and held me. His sudden care and concern was so out of character, I felt absolutely nothing except hate and contempt.

Then by some miracle, Mom got better. I truly felt the Creator had spared her, although I came to realize much later the sheer determination of her own spirit, especially when it came to me. Mom recovered in a couple of weeks, but she had a racking cough that lasted for months. As if nothing had happened, our lives went back to normal. Don still bullied her, slapping her whenever he felt like it. I begged her to leave him, but she was determined to make things work.

By now I had come clean about school, and in spite of Don's objections, I didn't go back. I found a job at McDonald's and worked there a couple of weeks before I quit. I went back to hanging out with my old friends, most of whom had dropped out of school. We drank and partied, hung out in the arcade or mall, shoplifting whatever we could take. I didn't see Aunty or Grandma Francis anymore. As far as I was concerned, being an Indian meant nothing — it had already caused too much trouble.

A week before Christmas, I got busted for stealing a leather jacket. When the cops hauled me home, Don exploded. Instead of hitting or grounding me, he kicked me out of the house. I had two days to find a place to live, and so by Christmas Eve, I was sitting on a bus heading to Salmon Arm, B.C., to live with Aunty Sandra and Uncle Tim.

Outside, the snowflakes were falling so thick and fast it was impossible to see a few feet ahead. Yet I felt safe, cocooned in this blinding white world. Finally I was free. Nothing from here on in could be as bad as living with Don. I had no idea what lay ahead, but the road, or so I believed, would be better. I opened the Christmas card that Mom had given me and read, "My darling Son, always remember that I love you. Take good care of yourself and I will do the same. Love always, Mom."

Twelve

First Passage

After the holidays were over, Aunty Sandra registered me for school, my sixth. In spite of having to repeat most of grade nine, I felt happy to be back in school, hopeful of my new beginnings.

I missed Mom terribly, worrying that something tragic, something final, would happen to her. Her near-death experience had affected me deeply, and in my mind she'd become a small child — my child — in desperate need of protection. I wrote her long letters, encouraging her to keep strong, always letting her know that I loved her, that I would do anything to help her. How loyal but naive I was, it seems to me now! I wanted so much to save her, to somehow give her the strength to leave Don.

I strongly believe my love of writing, my desire to communicate, came from those very letters. I recall labouring over the right words, the right sentiment. As I had done at the Spencers's, I poured everything I had into keeping our spiritual connection alive. I felt that if Mom could feel the "spirit" behind my letters, she would at least have something to hang on to, possibly even fight with. To this day, I approach the blank page with the "spirit" in mind. I believe that all good writing — writing that reaches into the heart and soul — comes from a sacred place, *our medicine place*, a place unmarred by convention or restriction, a place we all carry within.

While looking through Mom's things, I found many of my old letters. One letter in particular was hard to read, even after all these years.

March 12, 1981
Salmon Arm, B.C.

Dear Mom,

I pray that you are well and happy. Each night I ask the Creator to watch over you, to keep you safe and to give you strength. As for me, I'm okay. School is a lot better than it was at home. I've even managed to make some friends — pretty good ones, too. Aunty Sandra and I spend a lot of time together. We're more like friends. We can talk and talk and talk. I don't think Todd likes it too much. He's always picking fights with me. So far we've gotten into a few scraps, but nothing serious. Lisa's expecting her baby in the fall. She doesn't have much to do with anyone and I can't blame her. It gets pretty crazy around here sometimes, especially when Uncle Tim comes home.

Mom, I hope you're doing okay. I worry about you so much. I hate to think that you're alone down there. Never a day goes by that I don't think about you. I miss you so much. Do you ever hear my prayers at night? I may be here, but I'm always with you in spirit. I wrote a poem for you.

The snow has begun to melt, slowly disappearing
like a moth-eaten blanket.
Each day, I wake to see the sun
shining anew, shining triumphantly
through the bare maple trees, filtering
and falling like the robin's song
on the still frozen earth.

Soon will come spring
and all to life — life! Beautiful life!

What do you think? I wrote that yesterday morning before school started. Mom, remember that I love you. Keep strong, keep shining. Write soon.

Love Always,
Your Sun (Son), Greg

How hopeful I tried to sound, how optimistic despite the isolation and loneliness I felt! And yet I also recall feeling outrage towards Mom for staying with Don, for causing me anxiety and suffering. She was sick but she wasn't helpless. Why didn't she just tell him to fuck off, pack her things, and leave. Why on earth did she allow him to hit her? At least Aunty Sandra fought back when Uncle Tim was drunk.

In some innermost part of me, I understood Mom's fear, her inability to move forward. I, too, felt like a victim. My father, wherever he was, obviously didn't want me, nor did Don; Mom couldn't be with me because of him; Aunty Sandra and Uncle Tim took me in because I had no other place to go; Todd hated me because of it; the reasons went on and on. I felt my life up to this point was completely out of my control. I blamed everyone, mostly Mom.

Although I had made some friends, I hadn't a soul to confide in, except Aunty Sandra. I idolized her! She was everything that Mom wasn't. Although Uncle Tim hit her, she was tough and independent, with a no-nonsense attitude and biting humour. She found ways to fight back, even if it was taking off in the middle of the night with Lisa and me to Aunty Teresa's in Washington. Of course, Uncle Tim always came to get us and we ended up going back, but at least she stood her ground.

I understood Todd's dislike for me. How could I ever explain to him that I needed his mother's love, her strength, and optimism? She was all I had.

Two significant things happened while I was in Salmon Arm. At the time, I didn't give either of them a second thought, although each would affect my life's path and purpose.

I did much better in school here than in Coquitlam. I still struggled with math and science, but suddenly I took a keen interest in English, for it meant reading and writing, my two favourite things. Most of my classmates hated it, but I savoured the poetry of Keats, Milton, Wordsworth, Dickinson, and Browning. I especially loved Browning's "Child and the Watcher" and Milton's sonnets. Even more, I loved the writing assignments. I scribbled down poems and short stories as if a voice was whispering them in my ear. I filled so many notebooks, I didn't have to worry about having assignments to hand in.

My poems and stories gave me control of my universe, a universe that I had neither understood nor felt a part of, until now. Best of all, my feelings had come to life through my writing, and I felt as if I'd finally found a true friend, a friend with whom I could share everything.

Also, at long last, I took an interest in girls. I wanted so much to be like Todd: strong and athletic, manly and normal. I had always been quiet, silent — moving through life like a ghost, forever invisible, unseen, in the background. With the help of my friend Gene, I met more girls than I knew what to do with. In no time, I was taking them out to the movies or the roller-rink, holding their hands and necking with them. I couldn't help but recall one of the slogans I had heard at an AA meeting with Mom, "Fake it till you make it." I tried to be like the Fonz from "Happy Days," masculine and strong.

How painfully amusing it seems to me now. I was petrified of sex, more so intercourse. In fact, I did everything to talk my way out of it. My poor girlfriends! They were so willing to sacrifice their virginity. Yet no matter how heated our necking sessions, I felt like a fraud. I think I might have been more useful shopping with them or painting their toenails.

To this day, I feel ashamed and angry that I tried to be someone I wasn't. Even up until a few years ago, I refused to accept my sexuality. But I've come to realize that my years of confusion and struggle, like most gay people's, are rooted in society's disapproval and fear of homosexuality which cultivates, as it has done for generations, internalized homophobia and self-hatred. I also believe it is our experiences that make us strong. There is self-growth in everything, if we allow ourselves to be open to it. At fifteen, I wasn't open to anything, of course, except fitting in.

Towards the end of school, I met a girl named Tara, whose parents owned a hotel out on the highway. She was stunningly beautiful with long, wavy brown hair, big blue eyes, and a smile that could make even the toughest guy do cartwheels. Like all the other guys in school, Todd had his eyes on her, and I was sure she would fall for him. But surprisingly, she didn't notice Todd or anyone else. It was me that she liked. You can imagine the sheer triumph I felt. I had the admiration of every guy in school. I obviously had something they didn't. I wasn't sure exactly what that was, but I certainly wasn't going to start asking questions.

After I got over the initial shock of Tara's interest in me, I soon discovered that I truly liked her. She was nothing like my other girlfriends. She was genuine and concerned, interested in my life. I was able to confide in her, share my deepest fears and hopes. Oddly enough, I felt physically drawn to her, unlike my other girlfriends. Hidden in one of the hotel rooms, I read my poems to her: novice poems that began with lines like, "Hath love not speared my heart" or "Yearn thy heart for sweet kisses thou shall bring." I was in love! Head over heels in love!

But my great love was short-lived. Summer came, and by now Uncle Tim was home and drinking heavily. Up to this point, I had pretty much minded my p's and q's, drinking and smoking dope occasionally. But as things got worse, so did I. At every available opportunity, I sneaked booze out of the house. I spent the weekends with Gene (his mother was seldom home) and we got completely wasted along with our friends. Sometimes Tara came with me, but most times she left as soon as I got drunk.

I loved drinking, more so the world it put me in. I felt like a king — I ruled everything. But like Uncle Tim, I drank to the point of becoming aggressive. Suddenly I could do anything, say anything, no matter how ugly or mean. Where once I had vowed to never be like Uncle Tim, I found myself acting just like him. Half the time I couldn't remember what I'd done or said, even the scraps I had gotten into. Luckily, I never got stabbed or seriously beaten up.

Tara dropped me a short time later, but now I didn't care. There were plenty of girls around, all of them eager to join our wild parties.

Then one Friday night, my life came to a sudden halt. I was caught stealing a marijuana leaf from my cousin Lisa's photo album. Aunty Sandra told me that I had to leave. She sat me down and explained that I was old enough to be out on my own. The next day she took me to the bus depot. I had called Mom, and with Don's approval I was allowed to come home.

It took me a long time to understand Aunty Sandra's hard approach. At the time I thought she was so unfair and uncaring. But I came to realize her own situation was close to collapsing. The marijuana leaf was only an excuse to unburden herself, to somehow take control of her own uncertain future. I knew that she loved me as much as she loved my cousins. Perhaps she even felt that she was saving me, providing me with a chance to escape before something terrible happened.

What was I going home to? Had Don changed? My six months in Salmon Arm felt like a complete waste. Sure I felt older, more capable of looking after myself. But where would I go if Don kicked me out again?

While I was waiting for the bus, the strangest feeling came over me. It was as if I had been cut in two, separated into bad and good, ugly and beautiful, stupid and smart, hateful and loving. The notebooks in my duffle bag that held all of my poems and stories now seemed to belong to someone else. I walked around the back of the building, dug out the notebooks, and set them on fire. I watched them smoulder and burn, feeling absolutely nothing.

Thirteen

Seeds

Miraculously, finally, Mom left Don for good that summer. Despite the immense relief I felt, I couldn't bring myself to fully accept that the constant threat he had been to our lives was coming to an end.

I'll never forget his last night in the house. It is burned in my memory as if he'd planned it that way, as if he knew I was less afraid of him. If he couldn't be with Mom, then he was going to make me pay. Mom called me into her room and I distinctly remember her saying, "Greg, I know that things between you and Don haven't been the greatest. But I think it would be decent, manly of you to apologize to him." I couldn't believe my ears! Apologize to him? That son of a bitch! But Mom, with all good intentions, wanted a happy ending, so I agreed.

I stood outside his bedroom door, fumbling up the courage to say what my heart certainly didn't feel. I knocked and opened the door. Don lay in bed, seemingly engrossed in the newspaper. He didn't even look at me. "I — ah — just wanted to apologize for any trouble I might have caused."

Don didn't flinch. He kept on reading as if I wasn't there at all. I tried once again. "I know that you probably hate me and I — "

Don suddenly looked up from the newspaper, staring me down through his thick black-framed glasses. "Get one thing straight," he said. "If I ever catch you on the street, in a back-alley or anywhere alone, I'll break your arms and legs. Got it?"

I almost fell over. I felt as if I had just been given a death sentence, as if I had swallowed a black seed of poison that would eventually kill me. Don's words echoed inside my head. My days were now numbered, and I hadn't a hope in the world of escaping him. He would find me and beat me senseless, if not kill me.

I never told Mom about that night, instead allowing her to believe that I had done the "manly" thing. We moved into a small run-down house on the other side of town. It was owned by the municipality and was slated for demolition. Mom instantly loved it, drafts and all, saying that it reminded her of the old homestead in Whonnock. Both she and Grandma set to scrubbing it from top to bottom, repairing what they could. Yet another little shack with its peeling linoleum and cracked walls was transformed into a cozy home.

Outwardly, our lives appeared to be back on track. But we were both older. Mom had aged considerably. Her face was no longer soft but drawn and rough, furrowed with deep lines that made her look older. I, too, had aged, as if a painter had stolen in during the night and added dark circles beneath my eyes.

Over the next few weeks, Mom and I moved farther and farther apart. We argued constantly, forever blaming each other for the black shroud that hung over the house. Mom's drinking and pill-popping increased, and the less time I had to be around her, the better. She slept a lot, waking sometimes late at night only to fall back to sleep after picking at a sandwich or reading a chapter in one of her romance novels. Why did she give up now? We were away from Don, away from the bullshit. But she didn't seem to care about anything, including me.

I started grade nine again in the fall but dropped out two weeks later, staying long enough to have my picture taken for the school annual. I was now fifteen. Everyone else my age was in grade ten, close to graduating.

I started having nightmares about Don. These dreams filled me with terror, but also a certain amount of shame. He would be forever lurking in some dark recess, just waiting for me to stumble across his path. I would wake up covered in sweat, my breathing heavy, as if I had actually been running. Yet there were times in my dreams when I wasn't so lucky. He would catch me and choke me. I could feel the blood draining from my face, could see the stars shooting from behind my eyes, filling my head with blackness, a blackness that was strangely calm.

I often thought about death, the actual process of dying, and wondered what it would be like to be free of this horrible world. I imagined it to be eternally dark and quiet, nothing at all like heaven where angels supposedly sang and everyone was happy and free. To me, there was no such thing as heaven. There was only hell, the hell of life on earth.

November 25, exactly one month before Christmas, was a grey, miserable day. Mom and I were fighting because I refused to go back to school. I defiantly stood my ground, accusing her, too, of dropping out of life. We didn't speak the entire day, and by the time evening rolled around, I was tired of the tension. I went to bed early, wanting desperately to slip into oblivion. Mom's room was quiet and I assumed that she'd done the same.

I fell asleep shortly after midnight. I was dreaming of walking through a beautiful meadow, somehow knowing there was a river just beyond the tall grass. As I was nearing the riverbank, Don grabbed me from behind. "I've got you now, you little bastard!" he spat, and then he pushed my head under the water and held it there. I was screaming for Mom, but I knew she couldn't hear me. I was going to die. The water was filling my lungs and once again white stars were shooting from behind my eyes, and everything was turning black.

I awoke coughing, barely able to breathe. I lay in bed for a long time, shivering. The house was quiet and still. Mom had opened my door to let in the heat from the kerosene heater in the hallway. I got out of bed and sat down before it, staring emptily at the orange elements, trying to calm myself. A sudden well of emotion erupted within me. I felt small and helpless, ashamed of my weakness, my fear of Don.

Mom's bedroom door was also open, and I could hear she was sound asleep. I sat at the foot of her bed, listening to her breathing, wanting more than anything for her to hold me. I called her twice before I realized that she was in a deep, medicated sleep. I thought to myself, *It's just so like you to be dead to the fucking world, off in la-la land where nothing matters.*

There were various bottles of pills on the nightstand, and I examined each one closely, reading the labels in the glow of the heater. I didn't know much about pills, but I had taken Mom's valium before and so I figured it would do. At first I counted out twenty of the tiny blue pills, but then I decided I needed more. I counted out another twenty, went to the bathroom, and took them all in one handful. I scribbled a cryptic goodbye note and crawled back into bed. I lay there thinking about the past, happy that my crummy life would soon be over. At last I was going to be free.

I don't remember anything about the next two days. Years later I was told by Grandma (Mom refused to speak about it) that she found me late the next morning, dragged me to the car, and rushed me to Vancouver General Hospital. I came around enough to know that I was hooked up to intravenous. I also remember the doctors forcing me to swallow charcoal and a bitter-tasting liquid that made me vomit repeatedly. Although I was semi-conscious, I recall the look on Mom's face as she held the silver bowl under my chin. There was a tiredness about her that far outweighed my own. She looked absolutely beaten, broken beyond repair. As I was falling to sleep, I heard her calling to me from somewhere within a long tunnel. She was telling me to keep strong, to hold on to my dreams, to never let them go.

I awoke two days later in PAU, the Psychiatric Assessment Unit in the basement of the hospital. I was still pretty groggy, but more aware of the seriousness of the situation. A nurse helped me to the washroom, commenting that I was lucky to be alive. *Sure*, I thought to myself, *lucky for who?*

The unit was small and consisted of two separate sleeping wards, one for men and the other for women. The men's ward was painted a nauseating mustard colour and accommodated a dozen beds, all without curtain dividers. There was a common kitchen, dining area, and TV lounge where the patients, most of whom were old and senile, sat smoking one cigarette after another, mumbling things to imaginary people. The reception desk was also stationed in this area to allow the nurses full supervision of the unit. Behind that was the shower room, which like the main door was kept locked.

PAU was like a dungeon for crazy people, people who existed on a completely different planet. I was absolutely petrified of them, never knowing from one minute to the next what to expect. Besides me, there was another young person on the unit. She was Chinese, meek and timid, frighteningly quiet. I didn't know her name or why she was there, but I assumed it was for the same reason because her wrists were heavily bandaged. She never spoke to anyone or even looked at them. She walked around as if in a trance, completely oblivious to everyone.

One afternoon at suppertime I sat beside her. I was picking at my tray, wondering about Mom, when all of a sudden she jumped to her feet. She was stiff as a board and trembling all over, her eyes fixed on something that I couldn't see. She reached her hand up and made a sign of the cross. Then without warning she started to scream and vomited across the table. Two orderlies came rushing in and took her away. I never saw her again.

Four days had gone by and I was now fully conscious. I asked to go home, but was told no. I started to panic, thinking that

Mom had had me committed. I hadn't seen her and was growing more paranoid by the minute. Worse yet, what if she'd gotten back with Don? Then for sure I wouldn't be going home. He would see to that.

But a day later I was released. I was so happy, tears were streaming down my face, and I remember feeling much the same as when Mom had come to get me in Washington. My stay at PAU was a total of six days — six days that felt like an eternity. While I was there I had spoken to a few doctors, but refused to tell them why I had overdosed. I was afraid that they would call the social services and I would be taken away again. Instead, I made up answers to their questions. It was such a relief to hear the main door close and lock behind me. There was the smell of fresh snow in the air. Mom and I talked very little on the way home. We were both wrapped up in our own thoughts, our own suffering, I suppose. I vowed to myself that I would never again be so stupid.

Christmas was just around the corner and I busied myself with decorating the house, mostly for Mom. Grandma came to stay with us and everything seemed to get back to normal. Aunty and Chuck even made a point of dropping by often. Her stories and much-needed laughter filled the house.

Christmas and New Year's Day came and went quietly. Mom and I were getting along, this time both of us making an effort. When I told her about the dreams and the fear I had that Don would find me, she assured me that I was safe, and that she had no intention of getting back with him. We didn't talk about PAU or my overdose, and I was just as happy to forget about it as I knew she was. We planned to start over, take control of our lives. I was going to go back to school or look into an alternative program. Mom was going to cut down on her drinking, promising me that things would only get better.

But the second week into the new year, the phone rang. I remember the look of confusion, then anger, on Mom's face. It was her social worker, telling her that I had to go into a treatment centre for disturbed youth. I refused to have any part of it. But Mom said that we didn't have a choice, as the ministry would cut her off assistance if I didn't go. Her worker said that I was a danger to myself and to others, and that I needed to be hospitalized before anything else could happen. I panicked as soon as I heard the word *hospital*. How did the ministry know what was going on inside my head? I wasn't some sort of nutcase that needed to be locked up!

During the next few weeks I was like a prisoner counting the days until execution. Mom and I seldom spoke, and I felt like saying, *Oh great, here we go again. Thanks to you, my entire life is once again fucked up.*

The night before I was to leave, I contemplated killing myself. I would take the whole bottle of valium, if need be all of Mom's pills, and go into the woods where no one would find me until it was too late. I also thought about slitting my wrists like the Chinese girl. But in the end, I simply decided to go to the centre. I would keep my mouth shut, keep my thoughts to myself for as long as I had to. No one could force me to talk or tell them how I felt. My feelings were mine, no matter how ugly or frightening.

Fourteen

A Light in My Heart

At fourteen
I trusted men
the way a mouse
trusts a snake.
My dreams were phantoms
fluttering
bat's wings, mad cries
of my stepfather
lurching
from back alleys, dragging me
down dark streets
crushing bone, stealing breath.

The next morning as Mom and I drove into Vancouver, an unsettling silence stood between us. I felt as if I was the cause of her life's suffering, yet at the same time I felt completely betrayed, angry at her for her lack of nerve.

A wave of utter panic swept through me as we pulled into the parking lot of the Vancouver General Hospital. Unlike the first time, it appeared overwhelmingly cold and institutional. I thought about making a break for it, but where would I go? There was no escape from the social workers, the doctors, all of the people who controlled our lives. We were at their mercy.

The Adolescent Psychiatric Unit was not at all what I expected. It was considerably larger, more like a group home. The living room was spacious and comfortable, decorated with colourful wildlife pictures, a couple of overstuffed sofas and recliners, and a big-screen TV and VCR, complete with numerous video games and movies. The kitchen and dining room were combined into one big room. A large rectangular table and chairs accommodated the unit's fourteen residents and staff. Directly across the way was a small classroom which held desks and bookshelves, correspondence material, various books, and school supplies.

The reception area was located by the main door and was covered completely by plexiglass, as medication was dispensed there. A long hallway ran throughout the unit and on either side were offices and bedrooms. At the north end of the unit were the offices of the head psychiatrist and ward supervisor. Opposite the main door were two separate washrooms and a small, unfurnished, padded room, which I later discovered was the "time-out room."

After our tour we were greeted by Dr. McQuade, the head psychiatrist. He was typical of the doctors I had seen at PAU: middle-aged and balding, impeccably dressed. Though he seemed friendly and welcoming, I took an instant dislike to him. He led us to his office where we were introduced to the ward supervisor, a petite middle-aged East Indian woman named Nan Sharma. I shook her hand coldly and took my seat. She gave Mom a warm smile, shook her hand, and then directed her to the chair beside mine before introducing the rest of the group.

The two youth-care workers that had been assigned to my case were Michael DuBois and Carrie Smith. Both were in their mid-twenties and appeared friendly and eager to help *too* eager, I thought. Lastly, we were introduced to Ann, the school-teacher. She flashed us a polite smile, then focused her attention on Dr. McQuade.

Dr. McQuade rambled on for a good hour about the program, stopping periodically to ask if Mom or I had any questions. He finally finished and excused himself, saying that he had *other* patients to see. I remember thinking, *Yeah, like I signed up to be one of your God damn patients.* I hoped it would be the last I saw of him, and I could tell by the look on Mom's face she felt the same. She had told me numerous stories about her experiences with psychiatrists, none of them good. I resented how everyone in the room seemed to be looking at me and Mom. I was sure they saw us as poor welfare trash, more so Mom, as some sort of whacked-out pillhead who couldn't control me.

After Dr. McQuade left, the atmosphere in the room seemed to change. Nan stood up, smoothed out her lime-green sari and began to explain the ins and outs of the program. "The program," she began, "works on stages of behaviour. All new residents start on stage two, which allows you the privileges of the unit like watching TV or playing video games. You are allowed to wear your own clothes, eat with the other residents, and stay up until ten o'clock."

"The third stage," she encouragingly nodded, clasping her hands together like a saint, "means even more freedom. You are permitted supervised outings, the use of the phone, and are allowed visitors, primarily your Mom and family. Also, you are allowed to smoke, if you do."

"The fourth stage," she continued, "is a little more difficult to achieve, but with hard work and perseverance it can be accomplished. Once this happens, you will be allowed three hours of unsupervised time in which you can leave the unit. You must try," she cautioned, "not to get back-staged, especially to stage one. All of your personal belongings will be confiscated and you will be confined to your room in hospital pyjamas. As well, your phone privileges will be suspended and you will be required to eat in your room, *alone.*"

I felt as if she'd stressed the word "alone" as some sort of scare tactic, as if she was threatening me. I looked at her defiantly. "Well," I quipped, mustering up as much sarcasm as possible, "exactly how hard is it to move between the stages — and *exactly who* makes these *important* decisions?"

Nan cleared her throat and smoothed out the invisible lines from her lap. "The decisions," she said calmly, much too calmly, "are made by myself, Dr. McQuade, and the youth-care staff. We meet once a week to discuss your progress or *lack of it*." Her words hit the intended target, and I could feel the blood rush to my face. Mom reached over and squeezed my hand, but I was just as angry with her. Nan stood up and smiled, signifying the end of the meeting. The rest of the group remained seated. She asked Mom if she had any questions. Mom, looking as defeated as I felt, mumbled no. Nan followed her to the door, assuring her that everything would be fine.

Then like a flash, I suddenly realized Mom was about to leave — without me. They were already halfway down the hallway when I broke into a dead run. I reached the main door and had my hand on the push bar when I felt a powerful grip on my shoulder. I swung my fists wildly, screaming at the top of my lungs. But within a matter of seconds, I was wrestled to the floor by a large orderly.

Mom, Nan, Michael, and Carrie stood over me, silently bearing witness to my futility. I was so angry I couldn't even cry. Mom helped me to my feet and held me closely. She was crying and shaking badly, and I suddenly realized how much I loved her. She hugged me and whispered in my ear, "Greg, I am sorry. Whatever you do, play their games. Act like you don't know anything. Remember that I love you." I was completely astounded. It was the first time she'd ever apologized to me, seemed to comprehend the hopelessness of my life and how *I felt* about it. She kissed me and then disappeared out the door, which to my surprise locked automatically. I was trapped.

The first few days I spent a great deal of time in my room. I had been through a tiring succession of talking to doctors, doing their various tests, and I wanted to be alone. They always asked the same stupid questions, things like, "What do you fantasize about while masturbating?" or "Do you ever hear voices?" or "Have you ever thought about killing someone?" Of course I had thought about it, even felt like it. But I certainly wasn't going to tell them that. They would lock me up and throw away the key.

Yet, strangely enough, their questions left me feeling as if there was something truly wrong with me. I still thought about boys more than I did girls. And sometimes I heard Indian songs on the wind, sometimes voices, too. But they were good voices — voices of the Grandmothers and Grandfathers.

As the weeks dragged on and the tests became more difficult, I became more and more depressed. I kept thinking back to my overdose, wishing more than ever that I'd been successful. It was obvious that no one could be trusted, especially adults.

With a lot of coaxing from Michael and Carrie, I tried to mix more with the other residents. But I had nothing in common with them. Sure, they were just as fucked up as I was, but most of them came from good homes, had nice things and the attitude that went along with it. I viewed them as superior, much the way I thought about the kids at school. To me, they were spoiled white brats who had everything handed to them. They had no clue of the real world, let alone any idea of true pain and suffering.

I wasn't engaging with the other residents as was hoped by Nan and Dr. McQuade. I missed Aunty and the comforting smell of her house, the fresh bannock and apple pie she baked for me. I missed her stories and laughter, all the things that had given me such happiness when I was a little boy. Suddenly I felt small again, needful of her love and steady assurance. How I would have given anything to drift off to sleep to one of her Carter Family tunes!

Then one afternoon I was told that a special worker was coming to see me. She was a Native hospital liaison worker who dealt mostly with elders and people from up north. The following afternoon she came to see me. I instantly liked her. Rachel was Chilcotin from Williams Lake, in her mid-twenties, happy and unassuming, and full of jokes. Her dark eyes sparkled with a playfulness that put me completely at ease. She teased me about looking so white, saying that one side of the toaster must have been broken when I was born.

I gave her a tour of the unit and showed her some of my poems, which she read with great interest and appreciation, especially the ones about being Native. We talked for three or more hours and I told her everything. She didn't say a word or push me to tell her how I really felt, as the doctors had. Instead she listened patiently, encouraging me to keep talking. After our visit, I walked her to the door and she gave me a big hug as if she'd known me for years. She promised to come every week and I was overjoyed, feeling at long last I'd found a soul to confide in.

I recall one occasion when Rachel was unable to visit me. I was disappointed enough, without the added frustration of the unit. I became totally enraged when another resident made a racial comment about Indians being stupid and dirty. I retreated to my room and as usual tore up all of my poems, feeling ugly and worthless. After my fit was over, I slumped to the floor among the shredded paper and cried hysterically until I had nothing left. I pulled myself together and was straightening up when someone knocked at my door. When Michael walked in he was relaxed and smiling, which made me feel all the more embarrassed and stupid. He helped me clean up in silence and asked if I wanted to talk. I felt better, but wanted to be alone. I thanked him for his help and he hugged me, then left.

I thought about Michael that night. He was different from Don and Uncle Tim. He was gentle and kind, not the least bit threatening or intimidating. He had a sincerity, a realness that I could sense. Best of all, he knew when to pull back and give me space. There was also something else that I liked about him, something that I couldn't explain, although I found myself thinking about his blue eyes and rugged face. He was strong and tall, forever smiling with his eyes.

Nevertheless, I stayed clear of him for a couple of weeks. Sometimes I went with the other residents, mostly the girls, to the time-out room and listened to him play his guitar and sing. His voice was so beautiful that I couldn't even look at him. But I felt him watching me, singing loud and clear. By the time he finished the last chorus, my heart would be pounding, inexplicably aching. I would dash off to my room and write a poem about him, trying to capture the emotions he invoked in me, the beauty of his voice and how it had reached out and touched me. I would fly off to an imaginary place far beyond the wire mesh covering the windows, a place where Michael and I could be equals.

I began to feel more and more comfortable around him, and looked forward to his coming on to shift. I started to talk more, feeling safe and secure in his presence. *At last*, I thought, *there's a good man in the world — a man I can really trust.*

Even Rachel noticed a difference in me, commenting on my constant chattering and joking. I spent more time with the other residents, feeling a new and wonderful confidence. I even made a wholehearted attempt to get along with Nan, Dr. McQuade, and the other doctors.

Although I didn't fully understand it at the time, I knew that Michael favoured me. I could see it in his eyes and I could hear it in his voice. Often at bedtime, he came to my room and we would talk. He told me about himself and about his childhood in Quebec. He talked about his travels and his friends, and I thought he had a wonderful and exciting life. Although I missed my own life and freedom, his nightly visits somehow made my incarceration easier. I was amazed by his deep concern and understanding.

Already a month and a half had gone by, and without realizing it, I had adjusted to the flow of the unit. I started to deal with my anger, completely letting my guard down, allowing the doctors more insight into my head and heart. I was moving quickly through the stages, and I was a role model for newer residents. In fact, I was so comfortable with the routine that I dreaded going home, dreaded the thought of losing Michael. I had begun to feel safe, tingling with a new sense of myself — something that had to do with my heart and body.

One night, shortly after Michael came on to shift, something unexpected happened. I was already in bed, lying on my stomach, when I heard the door quietly open. Michael softly called me, and I knew without even looking at him that something was different. He crawled in beside me and started to rub my back. "You're so beautiful," he murmured. "I love the feel of your skin. It's so soft, so tight." He ran his fingers through my hair and nestled into my neck, his breath hot and heavy. I could smell alcohol. "You're so incredibly strong and mature," he groaned, "so different from the others."

Then without warning, he slipped his hand beneath my pyjama bottoms. I was absolutely frozen. He kissed the back of my neck and explored my body without speaking. I felt his body, his penis against me. "I've thought so much about kissing you," he confessed, turning me over so that our mouths met. He pressed his lips to mine and kissed me the way I had kissed my girlfriends, long and deep. I was petrified, and yet I felt joyously alive, pulsing like the blood rushing to my head.

Before Michael left, he told me that he loved me. He made me promise to keep *our secret*, half apologizing for his behaviour. I assured him that I wouldn't say a word, convinced it was just as much my fault. After all, I had dreamed about this night and written poems about it. I was older and more mature — at least that's what I wanted to believe. But inside I felt like a kid. I was suddenly afraid of our new relationship, afraid of the things he'd done and said. And I certainly didn't want him to know that. I wanted him to think that I was capable of making adult decisions.

Michael never mentioned that night, nor did we speak about it. I started to think maybe it was one of my crazy imaginings. But my body felt different. I felt nervous, yet oddly familiar in his presence. I looked for any reason to be alone with him, even if it meant acting out on purpose. But I also knew these were silly ploys, games that would make me look even more childish. Adults didn't act that way. And here I was, acting as if I was ten years old. I knew that I needed to be careful for Michael's sake. Nan and Dr. McQuade weren't stupid. Neither was Rachel.

As far as I knew, our secret was safe. No one suspected anything. Yet no matter how hard I tried, I found myself acting out in strange ways. I couldn't seem to help myself. I felt confused: destructively angry one minute and so in love the next. I felt as if Michael had tricked me, lied to me. Then again, I was sure that he truly loved me. Of course he couldn't openly display affection or come to me every night. An adult would understand that.

One afternoon, while I was writing, Michael came to my room. It was the first time in weeks that we were alone. He hugged and kissed me and apologized for his absence. He told me that he had a big surprise — he was going to take me out for supper. I was so excited, I threw my arms around him. Although I was on stage four of the program, I hadn't stepped foot outside the hospital, fearful that I might miss an opportunity to be alone with him.

Finally, seven o'clock rolled around and we left. Vancouver seemed like a brand new place. The lights were glimmering all around us and I pressed my face to the window of the car, drinking in the ambience of the city. Michael smiled at my excitement and reached over and kissed me.

We went to a busy café in the west end, and for the first time ever I saw men holding hands and kissing openly in the street. After supper we drove through Stanley Park and Michael parked the car near English Bay. We stood on the seawall, watching the lights shimmer and dance on the water. All around us there were high-rises, their windows aglow as if each suite held a party. I wondered where Michael lived — where I would live after I was released. He had promised to look after me.

Sensing my wonder, Michael took my hands and drew me close. "What are you thinking?" he asked, looking into my eyes.

"Oh, nothing. I'm just happy to be away from the unit."

He smiled and tightened his hold. "I think you've got the most beautiful lips — Indian lips," he said. He kissed me again, only this time there was an urgency about him. He pressed into me and I felt his excitement, his hunger. Unlike before, I, too, was excited. How I ached for him to take me home, to touch his naked body the way he had touched me.

On the way back to the unit I recall wondering about sex. I knew how to "do it" with girls, but boys were different. Besides the twins, I had no *real* idea what men did together. I thought about the time I had gone to stay with a friend of mother's when I was eight. I had to sleep with her son, Brian, who was seven years older. He had all sorts of dirty magazines. He was looking at them and touching himself. He wanted me to rub his penis, and so I did. Then he wanted me to put it in my mouth or bum, but I got scared and said no. I knew it was bad and told Mom. I wasn't allowed to go back there and I didn't see Brian until years later when his mother died. Even after all that time, I felt guilty, as if I had caused him a great deal of shame and trouble. And now it was the same with Michael. Only this time I was going to keep silent.

It was almost three months since my arrival at the unit. I was a model resident, doing all that had been asked of me. I had come out of my shell and received glowing reports from the doctors, Michael and Carrie, even Rachel. My anger, so they said, was more constructive and healthy. I was no longer a danger to myself or anyone else.

But secretly I felt terrible inside. I still trashed the love poems I wrote for Michael, ashamed of my feelings and desires, and sometimes, especially when I felt his attention slipping, I hit, scratched, or bit myself in private. I felt as if I deserved it, almost wishing that Don was here to beat me up. Michael seldom came to my room any more and it seemed he was trying his best to avoid me. I couldn't understand why. He'd said that I was beautiful, strong, and mature. He'd promised me happiness.

I began to realize that love was never without cost, that I forever ended up paying a heavy price — my heart and spirit — for a few moments of happiness.

Two weeks after our dinner, Nan told me that I was going home — home to Mom. How could Michael do this to me! I hadn't pestered him or acted out in any way. Most of all, I had kept our secret.

I was crying even before I got to my room. I started to hit myself in the face, disgusted by my own pitiful tears, ashamed of myself for trusting Michael. The more intense the pain, the more I cried, and the more I cried, the harder I hit myself. Then like a tornado, the rage turned outward. I smashed everything in sight, demolishing anything that wasn't screwed down. I tore the drapes down, ripped the blankets and sheets off the bed, and smashed the night-stand and rocking chair to pieces. I ripped up my poems.

The entire unit was buzzing around my door like frantic bees. Before I could do any more damage, I was restrained by two orderlies who gave me a shot and held me down until it took effect. I was losing all sense of time and space, but I knew Michael was nowhere around.

I awoke much later on the couch in the living room. Carrie sat beside me, scribbling notes on a silver clipboard. The unit was dark and quiet, and I wasn't sure if I'd been sleeping a couple of hours or a couple of days. Carrie fixed me something to eat and I ate in silence, trying to recall what I'd done. I wasn't sure if it had actually happened. My face was sore and I noticed my hands were swollen and bruised.

I suddenly remembered my outburst and asked Carrie about Michael. She looked at me for a long moment, offering up a hopeful smile. "Well, kiddo," she began, "he's leaving for Hawaii in the morning and he'll be gone for a month." My heart sank. Suddenly I wanted to tell her everything. But my anger was quickly replaced by emptiness. I retreated to that inner room that was mine alone, where no one could hurt me.

One week later I was released. It was determined, after intense observation, that my outburst was due to the anxiety I felt about going home. But inside I knew the truth and guarded it with my life, secretly hoping that Michael would come back for me. Every day I waited for him to call, even to say goodbye, but he never did.

I had written close to sixty poems in three months and had nothing to show for it, not even the memory of a favourite line, likely inspired by Michael.

Fifteen

Spirit-Keeper

an old woman was soothing me in Cree   I
cried in her lap   she kept singing   singing
an old man gave me four eagle feathers   four
songs   four stories   then painted my face
divided in two

It took me a long time to get over Michael, to forgive myself for trusting him. I suppose I still carry a certain amount of resentment towards him, as I do with most of the men from my younger life. But many of those long-ago pains are behind me. I have been able to find healing, to grow into the sort of man I so desperately needed as a child.

It disturbs me to think about the teenagers who, like me, experience this kind of introduction to the gay community. Michael not only violated a position of trust, but he scarred me deeply, shaped my image of gay men, myself, and the future. At one point, not so long ago, I believed the ultimate curse in life was to be gay. Sadly, Michael perpetuated the negative myth of gay men as predators, sexual perverts, and pedophiles.

Mom had no idea about Michael, nor was I going to tell her. I just couldn't bear to have her think Don was right about me being a "poofter." I struggled with my feelings in silence, moving through the days so deeply wounded, plagued by thoughts of suicide. Finally I couldn't stand it any more and wrote Michael a long letter, telling him everything I felt. I begged him to take me back, promising to love him until the end of time. The next morning I caught the bus into town and dropped the letter off at the hospital. I stood outside the door, uncertain as to whether I should give it to him personally or just leave it on the doorstep. I was afraid to see him and so I left it outside, hoping that only he would find it.

A few days later the phone rang and Mom answered it. By the look on her face, I was certain it was Michael. But it was Dr. McQuade. He had found the letter and read it. When he questioned me, I denied everything. All I could think about was protecting Michael. I wanted so much to believe that he still loved me. Dr. McQuade never called back, and as far as I knew the whole thing was dropped. Michael, of course, didn't call either. I never saw him again.

Years later I met one of the youth-care workers from the unit (he had restrained me the day of my outburst) who was teaching a workshop on Anger Management. I was working with young offenders, now a youth-care worker myself. After the workshop I introduced myself. He barely remembered me, but then I asked about Michael. His face grew pale and apprehensive and, without elaborating, he told me that Michael had left the unit shortly after I did, that he'd found a job with mentally challenged people. I later discovered (through Rachel) that he'd been bothering another Native boy at the unit.

So much of that time is a blur, but I do remember writing every day, even though I eventually destroyed my work. I wrote numerous poems and stories about being Native, wanting to connect myself to something spiritually nourishing, wanting to find some sort of belonging. The writing kept me alive, kept me somehow connected to an ancient world where I found peace.

While I was in the hospital, Rachel had encouraged me to find out more about my family background. I went to Salmon Arm to visit Aunty Sandra, and while I was there I wrote a letter to my grandfather's sister-in-law, asking if she had any information on the Scofields. She wrote back and told me about Kohkum Otter, the secrecy around Great-grandma Ida and the shame her children felt at being half-breeds. That letter made me feel very ambivalent. On one hand, I was happy to finally know the truth and, on the other, I was disappointed that we weren't *pure* Indians. I recall thinking that maybe Grandpa and his brothers and sisters were right to feel ashamed. Half-breeds were nothing.

After I returned home I showed Mom the letter, then threw it out, deciding to disassociate myself from anything white or mixed-blood. Kohkum Otter was Cree, so I was Cree, too. Oddly enough, I still thought of Mom and my aunts as white. How could I think of them differently? They certainly didn't seem interested in anything Native. I took a new interest in learning about the old ways — the Cree ways — and once again went to Aunty, who continued to teach me Cree and retold my favourite stories from my childhood.

One story was about *We-sak-e-jack*, the Trickster, and how he had tricked the ducks and geese into coming to his lodge for a special ceremony called the Blind Dance. Once the ducks and geese were assembled into a circle, *We-sak-e-jack* told them, "My brothers, this is a very sacred dance taught to me by my grandfather. You must keep your eyes tightly shut while I am singing, for if you open them, the medicine of this dance will be lost." And so *We-sak-e-jack* began to play his drum and sing. The ducks and geese danced in a circle, going round and round, their eyes tightly closed. But every now and then the drum would stop for no apparent reason. One little duck, who'd grown suspicious, decided to take a little peek. To his horror, he saw what *We-sak-e-jack* was doing. "Brothers," he cried, "*We-sak-e-jack* is killing us for his supper!" The birds took off in every direction, but *We-sak-e-jack* only laughed. "Blind Dance," he chuckled to himself. "Stupid birds!"

Besides going to Aunty for information, I also called Grandma Francis, and she, too, did her best to help me. As always she encouraged me to dance, letting me know where there were powwows and gatherings.

But the most significant thing that happened was a dream that was more like a prophetic vision. Some years later I wrote about this dream in my first book, *The Gathering: Stones for the Medicine Wheel*. The book begins with a story called "*Kiskey-tayew Maskwa Osisima*" (Black Bear's Grandson). I originally changed the story so as not to give away the *power* of my vision. But I now feel I can share it as part of my sacred journey, a journey predestined by my grandmothers and grandfathers.

Aunty told me that, long ago, young boys were sent out into the wilderness on their first vision quest. They were required to fast and pray for four days, thus cleansing their minds and bodies to receive a guardian spirit that would lead them through life. My dream was much like these vision quests. It began in an old cemetery somewhere in the wilderness. Among the carved headstones and crosses there were totem poles that seemed to reach the sky. Some of them held mortuary boxes where the bones of ancient people had been laid to rest.

There were other boys with me in the dream, all the same age. Some of them appeared anxious and impatient while others, like me, were scared and unhappy. An old man, whom we called Grandfather, gathered us together and began to talk to us. "Grandsons," he began, "today is a very sacred day, for today you are no longer boys but men. Some of you are old in spirit and some of you are still very young. Some of you," he continued, pointing to the mortuary boxes, "do not come from here, but these are the bones of your grandmothers and grandfathers. You are about to embark upon a very sacred journey. If you become scared, think of them, for they will help you. They will give you strength. Some of you will become lost and frightened. Look within your heart and there you will hear a sacred song. Sing it and you will again find your way.

"Grandsons," Grandfather instructed, "you are to go towards the east, the Place Where All Life Begins. Along your journey you will meet a black bear. Do not be afraid of him, for he, too, is your grandfather. Approach him respectfully, and if your heart is good, he will let you pass. He will give you medicine."

As we started out, the sky grew dark and claps of thunder rolled in the distance. Soon we became separated, and I found myself wandering alone in the dark forest. It began to rain, and peals of lightning tore across the sky, illuminating the treetops. I became hopelessly lost, feeling angry and frustrated. I started to cry, thinking that I would never find my way. But then I remembered the bones of the Grandmothers and Grandfathers. I sat down on a fallen tree, closed my eyes, and listened to my heart. Suddenly, I heard the song. How beautiful it was! I could hear the Grandmothers singing high above the Grandfathers, their voices strong and powerful.

I started out again, singing, only this time I felt as if my feet were being led by an invisible force. Soon it was morning. I walked and walked until I reached a small clearing. There in the distance, I saw the black bear. My heart felt as if it was going to stop beating, but I approached him respectfully.

As I stood before him, Grandfather Black Bear stood up on his hind legs and looked deeply into my eyes, and I felt him say to my heart, *Grandson, you have nothing to fear. Your heart is good and you have much work to do. Go now and do not look back.* He fell down on all fours and ambled off into the forest. I began to run and my body suddenly felt light and graceful. As I ran faster, my feet lifted off the ground and I began to fly. I flew above the treetops, looking down upon our little shack and myself sleeping in bed. I awoke with the sacred song in my head.

As I wasn't on a vision quest, at least in the physical sense, I'm not certain why I was given this dream. But this is not for me to ask. I believe *Kee-chee-manitow*, the Creator, touched me in a sacred way, gave me power I would need later on. Although I have lived in many places and done many things since my vision, it is still as vivid to me today as it was sixteen years ago. I have been given Bear Medicine — healing medicine — and I honour this medicine by writing. I believe this is what Grandfather Black Bear meant when he said, *You have much work to do.*

I went back to school in May. The Native Education Centre was like heaven compared to public school. It was an adult basic-education program in Vancouver that provided upgrading and cultural/spiritual courses for urban Native people. The entire program, except for math, was taught from a Native perspective, using the works of Native writers and spiritual people. As well, there were classes in beadwork and leatherwork, hide-tanning and drum-making, classes on powwow singing and dancing, and even traditional Native cooking.

Most of the students were older, some of them Mom's age, married or shacked-up with families. At first, I felt awkward because of my age, but I soon realized it didn't matter. Everyone treated me as an equal, more so than I'd ever felt in public school. I was excited to be with my own people and to meet students from tribes from across Canada: Nishga'a, Haida, Salish, Blackfoot, Mohawk, Cree, and Ojibway. To some degree, we were all displaced people, survivors who had either been through foster care, in jail, or on the streets. Some of the students had lost their children to social services or had come out of abusive, drinking relationships. All of us were struggling to heal the past, to find some sort of meaning in who we were.

Most of the teachers were white but sympathetic to the Indian cause, even somewhat radical. I began to learn about people like Anna Mae Aquash, Leonard Peltier, Dennis Banks, and Russell

Means, about the political battles and injustices they and other American Indian people suffered at Wounded Knee in the late seventies. I also began to learn about Canadian Native history: the truth behind the government's broken promises and the residential schools — all of the information that was avoided in high school.

I remember one teacher in particular, whom almost everyone admired and respected. Peter was from Chicago and supposedly Native, although it was rumoured he was Jewish. I didn't care either way because he was a good teacher, more so because everything he taught had a political agenda. For English and social studies he encouraged us to debate his opinions, many of which were from a Eurocentric perspective. Of course, he did this on purpose, but some of the students took it to heart, practically coming to blows with him. Nevertheless, his "fire-starter" teaching style hit the mark. Many of us would be close to armed resistance by the end of his class.

Now Mom and I seemed to reach a new level in our relationship. She treated me more like an adult, often talking to me about her feelings and childhood experiences. She even took an interest in some of the things I was learning, primarily the political struggles of Native people. We would have long conversations about some of the books I brought home. She seemed genuinely interested, and I started to see her differently. How, I wasn't sure, although I found myself including her more in my newfound awareness.

A short time later I moved out on my own. I found a small attic suite close to school in the house of an older German couple. They were apprehensive at first because of my age, but I promised to be responsible, clean, and quiet. Because I was too young to get welfare, Mom paid the rent and gave me grocery money out of her cheque. The ministry didn't know, and so they continued to pay for my tuition and school supplies, but that was all. If I needed anything else, I went to Mom.

When school let out, I found a summer job with a Native theatre company called Spirit-Song. The program was for Native youth and was meant to teach us theatrical training and work skills. The director was a well-known Native actress, who for some reason disliked me. She made me feel out of place and untalented, as if I was wasting her time.

I became more and more self-conscious of my appearance, doing what I could to fit in. I dyed my hair black and spent every available minute in the sun. Thankfully, my skin had a bit of dark pigment and I was able to turn nut brown. The only thing I couldn't change was the colour of my eyes. Oh, how I hated having grey eyes.

I devoted myself to Spirit-Song, to becoming a great actor. I was excited by our upcoming tour of the legend pieces we'd been rehearsing, various West Coast legends that we had adapted for the stage. I played the Seagull in the Haida legend *How Raven Stole the Sunlight*. The main character was, of course, the Raven, played by an actor whom I secretly envied for being *more* masculine and Native looking. As the story went, he steals the sun and keeps it hidden in a box. My character, the flamboyant Seagull, somehow tricks him and saves the world from eternal darkness. It wasn't a glamorous role, but it was a funny one.

We were scheduled to perform at a Native theatre festival on Vancouver Island in July. I went to the beach every day after work and studied the seagulls for hours. I was determined to upstage the Raven. The Native community would love me and the director would see that I was talented and worthy of her time.

Sixteen

Second Passage

Falling in love was the farthest thing from my mind that summer. But Kevin was a dream come true, tall and fair, with light brown eyes, which was unusual for a B.C. Indian. He was from a remote village along the West Coast and, like his brother and two sisters, had moved to Vancouver in the hopes of finding a better life. He was twenty-eight and soft-spoken; I couldn't imagine him ever getting into a fight.

I met him the night of my seventeenth birthday and immediately fell in love with him. He was different from Michael, from anyone I'd ever met. He was polite and unassuming, and I felt as if I'd known him for years. He was with a friend named Veronica, who was a friend of Tracy's, a girl from school, who I had moved in with. It was obvious that she was in love with him, for she hung on his every word. Despite her constant joking, I knew she was jealous of the interest he showed in me.

The party ended early and Tracy and her friends went to the bar, leaving the three of us alone at the apartment. We smoked some dope and went to the beach. Kevin sat beside me and held my hand, occasionally leaning over to kiss my cheek. It seemed so magical, everything except Veronica who kept clearing her throat and sighing disgustedly. Later we went back to the apartment and slept on the floor. Kevin arranged it so that I was in the middle, next to him. Veronica huffed and accused him of being a pervert, saying that I was too young for him. Finally after she fell asleep, he held and kissed me. I went to sleep in his arms, feeling a different kind of safety.

Looking back on that night, I realize how naive I was, and how, like Veronica, I wanted so desperately to be loved. I wanted to laugh and kiss like all of the men I'd seen on Davie Street. I wanted to feel good about myself. I was tired of feeling ugly and ashamed, tired of trying to be someone I wasn't.

The next morning when the theatre company left for Vancouver Island, I could barely concentrate on the performance. We arrived in Campbell River a couple of hours before the show and I hurried off down to the beach, practically floating over the wet rocks and driftwood. I found a tail feather from a bald eagle and was overjoyed, believing it to be some sort of sign. I held it to the sky and thanked the Creator for sending me Kevin.

Apart from our collective nervousness, the show was a great success. Afterwards, we went to the community hall and feasted on salmon, smoked halibut, seaweed, oolican grease, and frybread. The elders praised us, making us promise to come back. They congratulated the director for her hard work and gave her all sorts of beautiful gifts.

On the way home, I sat across from her on the ferry. I was deep in thought, daydreaming about Kevin, when suddenly I caught her watching me. She cleared her throat, her dark eyes narrowing to slits.

"You certainly don't look very Native," she said flatly. I shrugged my shoulders.

"I mean, look at you" — she glared at me — "you've got grey eyes and blond eyelashes."

"Well," I hesitated, "I was born that way." She was silent for a moment and then her face grew even colder.

"Well, you'll never get cast in a Native role."

After we got back to Vancouver, I decided to quit. I was making a fool of myself acting in a Native play. People were probably laughing at me, saying, *Look at that white guy up there. No wonder he's playing the Seagull.* I didn't go into work the next week. The director kept calling me. Finally I couldn't leave it any longer and decided to face her.

"Greg, you can't just quit," she argued, "we've got three more shows. What about the cast?"

"I can't stay. I'm not a good actor and — besides, the program is almost over."

"Look! We've got three more shows and *you're in them*!"

"No!" I was quick to answer.

"Fine!" she shrugged, "if you walk out of here, don't expect to come back. And don't expect," she added, "to get a reference from me!"

I got up to leave. "I may look white," I said bluntly, "but you fucking well act it!"

It was one of the first times in my life I said how I truly felt. Although I no longer had a job and was dependent upon Mom again, I didn't care. I was proud of myself.

The next few weeks I saw Kevin practically every day. I met his sister, Rose, and her six-year-old daughter, Becky, whom he lived with in a low-income housing project on the downtown eastside, an area known for its rejected people, heavy drug use, violence, and high death rate. I was soon going over for supper and staying the night while Kevin babysat. Rose was usually gone, but sometimes I ran into her as she was leaving. She would be dressed in tight miniskirts and high heels, all made up and smelling of perfume. At first I assumed that she had a boyfriend, but Kevin later told me that she was a prostitute. I felt awful for her, but more so for Becky. Would she have the same kind of life that I had endured?

I knew that Rose drank and did drugs, and it seemed understandable given the situation. But a lot of the time, Kevin got stoned with her, sniffing cocaine or dropping acid. Usually Becky and I sat in front of the TV while he dozed in and out of consciousness. Finally I would drag him off to bed and tuck Becky in, telling her stories about *We-sak-e-jack* and the animals. For the first time I was part of an adult world and its ugliness, feeling responsible for Becky and yet helpless to do anything.

Up to this point I hadn't thought about the age difference between Kevin and me. But more and more, it was evident that he saw me as a kid. We hadn't had sex, at least not fully. We slept together naked and kissed, but that was it. For the most part, he was usually too drunk or stoned to do anything. And yet I didn't mind. I was happy just to lie with him, relish the moments of security I could find.

When school began in September I was glad to get back to the cultural activities, political discussions, and books. One book I remember was Maria Campbell's *Half-Breed*. It proved to be one of the most important books of my life, although at the time I didn't think so. I was even angry at Peter for making me read it. Worse yet, I had to write a report on it.

I recall the day he handed the book out in class. I took one look at it, saw the title, and set it aside. I thought it was irrelevant to who we were as Indians, and told him so. But he insisted it was just as important as the Anna Mae Aquash book. I threw it in my knapsack, thinking, *What could some half-breed woman possibly have to say?*

I laboured over her story. I even threw the book across the room a couple of times. Her life seemed so hopeless, so full of misery and suffering. I felt as if she was somehow describing Mom and Aunty Georgie, even me, and I hated her for it. Most of all, I hated her for telling the truth. By the time I had finished writing my report, I felt so full of rage. An inexplicable rage at everything — at Mom, at Aunty, our poverty, my grandfather's shame, my own shame. I put the book in the trash can, handed in my report and forgot about it. I was Cree — not some forgotten half-breed who didn't belong anywhere.

One weekend I went to stay overnight with Kevin. To my surprise, he was sober and Becky was already asleep. He made some popcorn and we curled up on the couch to watch a movie. Before I knew it, we were necking. We went to his room, stripped off our clothes, and made love. It was so unbelievable, I felt like a real adult.

We found an apartment a few weeks later. I was excited that we were finally going to be together. I told Mom that I'd found a new roomate through school. I made up my mind that nothing was going to spoil my dreams, even if Kevin drank or did drugs occasionally. He promised to slow down and I promised not to overreact if he went out with his friends.

I knew that his friends didn't like or approve of me. They teased him constantly, calling him a "chicken hawk" or "old troll." Whenever I was around them I tried to act older, funny, and smart. But mostly I kept to myself, sitting in the corner, watching them carry on. They did a lot of drinking and drugging and, like Kevin, the more they drank the more self-conscious I became.

Because our apartment was in the east end of the city, it was dangerous to go out alone, especially at night. Every few days on the news there were reports that someone had been raped or killed in our neighbourhood. The complex was huge and made entirely of cement. It looked like a derelict castle, perched on the side of a steep hill. All sorts of people lived there: a lot of new immigrants, but mostly drug addicts, dealers, and drunks. The hallways and elevators smelled of stale beer, urine, and unwashed bodies, and no matter how many times they were cleaned, it didn't seem to make a difference. It reminded me of the old apartment in Maple Ridge.

Our suite was large and fairly clean, although the kitchen and bathroom swarmed with cockroaches. The living room was bright and spacious, with a big window and balcony that over-looked Grouse Mountain, but the carpet was filled with ciga-rette burns. The bedroom was also large and bright, only the walls were paper-thin and we could hear the tenants next door, who seemed to party non-stop. But none of this mattered. As long as I was with Kevin, I was happy.

Rose often used our place on the weekends to bring her "dates." I wasn't sure of the arrangement she had with Kevin, although I suspected she gave him money or drugs in exchange for using it, and for babysitting. In spite of the dirtiness I felt, I kept my mouth shut, afraid that he would accuse me of judging her and leave me.

Kevin was on welfare and the small amount I received from Mom barely paid the rent. All month long we'd practically starve, relying on food vouchers or the food bank. I felt humili-ated standing outside the welfare office or Friendship Centre. I tried to encourage Kevin to get a job or go back to school, but he wouldn't. Then cheque day would roll around and we'd be flush for a little while.

By the time five months had passed, Kevin had completely changed from the man I'd fallen in love with, the man I believed him to be. He didn't seem to care about anything, and his promises meant nothing. As soon as he got his cheque, he'd be gone for a couple of days, sometimes even a whole week. I tried to keep calm, but each passing hour felt like an eternity. Finally I would go downtown to look for him. As usual, I found him in the bars with his friends. He was usually so drunk or stoned that he couldn't recognize me. Other times, he was nursing a hang-over and would yell at me to fuck off, screaming that I was stupid, forever threatening to leave me.

Well into my twenties, I believed that Mom had no idea about Kevin or our relationship. I was so ashamed of myself I couldn't face her, let alone tell her the truth about the lifestyle I had chosen. If she did know or suspect anything, she certainly kept it to herself. Years after her death, I often found myself talking to her about my failed relationships, mostly about the great loneliness and hopelessness I had felt. I have since grown enough to know that she loved me deeply, that she would have accepted me regardless of the choices I made. I remember her words, which now express so clearly her unconditional love and acceptance: "Darling, I don't care who you love, just as long as you're happy and safe."

Aunty also knew nothing about Kevin, or so I believed. Sometimes she and Chuck came into town and stopped over after bingo. Her visits were a godsend. I could be young and carefree again, lose myself in her stories just as I had when I was young. So many times I wanted to tell her how unhappy I was. But like Mom, I was afraid to tell her the truth, afraid that she would stop loving me.

At some point, I began to attend Native Family Night, which was held every Monday at a local Neighbourhood House. It was like a mini powwow, but mostly people came to socialize over tea and bannock, listen to the drum groups, and watch the dancers. Kevin refused to come with me and made fun of the whole thing. But I didn't care. In fact, I was even relieved, as I didn't want anyone to suspect anything. Besides, it was a good opportunity to get out of the apartment, take some time away from him. I could feel proud and good for a couple of hours.

Kevin seldom talked about being Native or growing up on the reserve. When he did, he was drunk and talked mostly about his mother, who had raised the kids almost single-handedly. He hated his father as much as I hated Don. He told me that his father was an alcoholic and that he'd physically and sexually abused all of them.

One time I asked him if his mother knew he was gay. To my disappointment, he hadn't told her, although he said if and when he did, it wouldn't make a difference. Suddenly a light went on in my head. His mother had the power to make things go right, and I was determined to meet her. I was sure, without a doubt, she would like me, maybe even love me. After all, I loved her son and was willing to do anything to make him happy. All I had to do was try harder, be patient, and wait.

But little by little my hopes gave way to reality. Kevin only got worse, taking off for weeks at a time. I was so depressed I could barely get out of bed in the morning. Everything seemed dead. Death, whether real or emotional, is like a thief who steals in during the night, robbing you of everything. I tried to keep up with school, but even that was hard to manage. Worse, our rent had fallen behind and there was no food. I swallowed what little pride I had left and went to welfare. But I was denied help because of my age, and told to go home. I called Mom, telling her as little as possible. She borrowed some money from Grandma, but still it wasn't enough.

The rent was due again and the phone company was threatening to disconnect the line. I had only a few dollars left of the money Mom had given me. Kevin was nowhere to be found, and I decided I was getting out. To add to everything, we were given an eviction notice; we had five days to vacate the suite. I was determined not to go home because I knew I would be equally miserable there.

Suddenly I started thinking about Rose. At first the whole idea of selling my body, having sex with strangers, repulsed me. I thought of them groping me, forcing my head into their laps. But I closed my eyes and imagined my very own place filled with beautiful things: the cupboards and fridge stuffed with food; the closets crammed full of expensive shoes and clothes.

I went to the bedroom, pulled open the closet doors, and started rifling through Kevin's clothes. I found a turquoise mesh tank top and slipped on a pair of white Levi's and runners. I sprayed on some of his cologne and took one last look at myself in the mirror. What would Mom, Aunty, and Grandma Francis say? I rushed out of the apartment before I could even think about it. On the way downtown I kept telling myself, *Don't think. Whatever you do, don't think.*

"Boystown" was one of the loneliest places I'd ever seen. It was tucked in behind huge high-rises and office buildings, dimly lit by street lamps. The hustlers stood in darkened doorways in groups of two or three, fervently looking into the windows of cars as they passed by. Most of them were my age and looked as if they'd been kicked from one end of the earth to the other.

I took a spot on the opposite side of the street where no one was standing. I knew that they were all watching me, wondering who I was. I could see them talking, and was scared to death that they were going to beat me up. Finally one of them came over, a good-looking blond boy who wore a white tank top and baggy jeans.

"Hey, dude, what's up?" he said, looking me up and down. "You working, or do you wanna date?"

"Working," I mumbled.

"What's your name?" he asked, fumbling in his pocket for a cigarette. He offered me one and lit it.

"Greg."

"I'm Gerad," he nodded, leaning into me, holding his crotch. "Got any rigs?"

"What's that mean?" I shrugged, feeling stupid. He grinned and shook his head.

"You know, needles."

"I don't do that," I said.

"Hmm," he nodded skeptically. "We're all good girls, too —" he looked around. "Good thing the fashion police haven't been around. You look like a fucking virgin. And don't tell me your mother dressed you."

He gave me a dirty look and pointed to a spot down the street.

"See the Murchies Coffee sign?"

"Ya."

"Well, go and stand there. This is my fucking spot."

Being new to the stroll, I had absolutely no idea how to get "dates" or even what to charge them. I stood under the Murchies Coffee sign and, like the rest of the hustlers, waited. There was such a lump in my throat, I couldn't even swallow. I was so distraught, I didn't even notice a car had pulled up beside me. It was an older guy, gesturing for me to come over.

"I'm looking for some company," he smiled seductively, motioning for me to get into the car. I froze.

"I'm looking for some *company*," he said more insistently. I stood there, blindly staring into the car, trembling all over.

"Look, honey, are you interested or not!" he yelled.

"Go fuck yourself!" I screamed, more at Kevin than him.

He sped off and the other boys down the street were looking at me as if I was crazy. I pulled myself together and went home. I couldn't do it, even for money.

Seventeen

The Weight of Belonging

The apartment was just as dark and empty as before. The eviction notice sat on the kitchen counter where I'd left it, and cockroaches scurried back and forth as if nothing mattered except the few wayward crumbs beneath it.

Time was running out. We had only a few days left to pack our things and move. I went to the washroom, pulled open the medicine cabinet, took out the bottle of tylenol and swallowed as many pills as I could stomach. I took one last look around the apartment, praying now that Kevin wouldn't come home. I didn't want him to know what I'd done. I didn't need his apologies or pity. I just wanted it all to end.

I lay on the couch for a long time and watched the lights of Grouse Mountain shimmer in the distance. I dozed off and on, replaying the scenes of my relationship with Kevin: our first meeting and how he'd held and kissed me; the nights we'd lain awake talking and laughing; the many times he'd left me and the hundreds of things that I'd never said. I tried to put everything into perspective, but my mind wandered so badly I couldn't make sense of anything. I found myself floating back into the past, back to the days of my childhood, listening to Aunty's stories. I thought about Mom and all the years of separation and pain, and I asked the Creator to watch over her.

I felt as if I had swallowed sand, and my eyes were sore and heavy.

I'm really going to die this time, I thought. *I'm dying and I'll never get another chance at life.*

Then, pulling myself up, I remembered Mom's words after my first overdose: "Suicide is a quick and easy answer to a temporary problem." Suddenly I felt determined to fight, to find a solution. Nothing mattered now: not the past or Don or Michael, not Kevin or the eviction notice.

I called a taxi and went to the hospital. I told the doctors what I had done, and begged them not to call Mom. They forced me to vomit, and after my stomach was empty I fell into a deep, dreamless sleep. After seeing the hospital psychiatrist in the morning, I was allowed to go home.

The apartment was still empty. I crawled into bed. All I wanted to do was sleep. I shut my eyes and prayed, *Creator, if you really exist, then help me. Please help me.* I awoke sometime in the early evening to discover that another eviction notice had been pushed under the door. Tomorrow we had to be out, and the phone was being cut off. I contemplated calling Mom, but then I suddenly remembered Yvette Jonas from Family Night, her invitation to call her if ever I needed help or a place to stay.

I didn't know much about Yvette or her family, only that she was Tlingit and worked at the Neighbourhood House as a Native family worker. She was close to Mom's age, but she looked younger, with waist-length black hair, dark eyes that seemed to look into your soul, and a serious but kind face etched with soft lines. She was married but didn't have any children. She and her husband Perry lived in a big house in south Vancouver, which they shared with her brothers and sisters, and their spouses and children.

Yvette was well respected by the people who attended Family Night because she was kind and caring and full of good advice.

She followed the Indian way and seemed to help anyone in need. She had organized the Family Nights and encouraged the young people to dance.

I called Yvette and explained my situation. But I was afraid to tell her about Kevin. Instead I told her that he was my roommate and that he'd taken off without paying the rent. I was also afraid to tell her about my overdose and Boystown. She said that I could stay with them, and made arrangements for her brother and nephew to help me move.

Later on that evening, as I was packing, Kevin came home. I took one look at him and burst into tears. I had so much to say, but I didn't know where to start. Besides, it was useless now. Our relationship was over. He tried to hold me, but I pushed him away. I felt so betrayed and angry. And yet I still loved him.

I moved into Yvette's house the next day. The house was one of the largest I'd ever seen. There were three bedrooms upstairs, a washroom, large living room, dining room, and an even larger kitchen. Yvette's older brothers, Sam and Tony, slept upstairs, as did her sister Monica, her husband Dave, and their son Kyle, who was a few years younger than I was. There were also three bedrooms downstairs, a rec-room, washroom, and small kitchen. Yvette and Perry, her sister Donna and her daughter Tammy, her brother Les, and I slept downstairs. A lot of the time other family members came to visit, and the couches and floors would be full of people.

The house was filled with old furniture and decorated with family pictures and Native posters. In the rec-room there was a sewing machine, boxes of material, and bags of scrap leather and fur. On the coffee and end tables sat plastic margarine tubs full of shiny beads, needles, and various sewing items. Every available space was occupied by someone's craft project, whether it was a pair of moccasins, earrings, or dance regalia.

At first I found it difficult to be around so many people. I wasn't used to communal living. Whenever there were any problems, everyone seemed to know. Yet no one ever talked about them. They kept quiet, moving around the house like ghosts, their heads down, as if a tragedy had befallen them. Yvette usually dealt with these problems, and I soon realized that she was in charge of the household.

The first couple of months were hard. I went for long walks and rethought the past, trying to sort everything out. Sometimes I even went downtown to look Kevin. But I never found him. I tried to show a happy face to the family, but Yvette knew something was wrong. She often asked my about my *sadness*, but I still couldn't bring myself to tell her the truth.

A short time after I moved into the house, I discovered more about Yvette and her family. All of them had been taken from their home reserve as children and sent hundreds of miles away to St. Joseph's Mission School in Williams Lake. This school was one of the worst in Canada, notorious for physical and sexual abuse by the nuns and priests. They never talked about their experiences, although each of them had suffered a great deal. Most of them had spent time on the streets and had battled alcoholism and drug addiction.

At some point the family became involved with the Native Church of North America. A combination of Christianity and traditional beliefs, it celebrated Christianity through what was called the "Peyote Sacrament" and sought to teach its followers "morality, sobriety, industry, kindly charity, and right living." The peyote was used for both medicinal and ceremonial purposes. When eaten, it enduced relaxation, euphoria, and psychedelic trances in which vivid images appeared.

Most of the family "meetings" were held outside of Vancouver and began on a Saturday evening. They were held in a tipi with the door facing east. The meetings began at sundown, after a sweatlodge ceremony, and lasted until full daylight on Sunday. There were breaks at midnight and dawn.

Everyone usually sat in a circle flanking Sam, the "Road Man," who faced the door. The women sat on one side of the tipi and the men sat on the opposite side. A central fire was lit in front of a low mound of sand that served as the altar; nearby were a water drum, gourd rattle, staff, and eagle feathers used to accompany singing (done by the men) as the peyote was passed around. On the altar itself was placed a large peyote button known as "Grandfather Peyote."

There were four main jobs in the lodge. The Road Man conducted the meeting, ensuring that everyone stayed awake and sat upright. Dave, the "Fire Chief," kept the fire going, moving the embers closer to the altar as the evening progressed. Perry acted as the "Doorman" and was responsible for watching anyone who needed to leave the tipi. He was also responsible for taking the "sickness" out of the lodge. Peyote is very nauseating, and vomiting is considered a part of purgation. Lastly, Yvette or one of her sisters was responsible for bringing in the morning water. They prayed over it, asking the Creator to bless everyone in attendance.

My very first meeting was held downstairs in the house. The windows were covered with heavy blankets, the furniture was moved, the doors were locked and the phones unplugged. As usual, the meeting was held on Saturday evening and began at sundown. When the fireplace was cleaned out and a fire was kindled, Sam arranged the altar in front of it, laying out the cere-monial objects and Grandfather Peyote. Everyone took their designated seats on the floor and the lights were turned out. We were each given a large bowl and told to use it if we felt sick.

Sam prayed for a long time and then the water drum was passed to Dave. Kyle sat beside him and stood up on one knee, holding the gourd rattle and staff. Dave began to hit the drum. The steady beat was deep and hollow, haunting as it reverberated against the walls. Kyle shook the rattle in unison, and then he began to sing. The song was unlike anything I'd ever heard before: *Hiya-nee-he-na-he-no — Hiya-nee-he-na-he-no — He-ya-no-hay-hay.*

Kyle sang three more songs, and the peyote was passed around. It had been cooked into a thick slushy mush and then mixed with water. We each took a tablespoon of the mixture and ate it with sage tea, which tasted bitter and awful. Sam invoked more prayers and then the drum was passed to Perry. Sam sang four more songs and the peyote was passed around again. This went on throughout the night, and each time I ate the peyote I felt more and more sick.

At times I felt as if I was floating around the room. The hollow sound of the drum, the wild and hypnotic singing was unearthly. My head felt as if it was about to explode, and my eyes were burning so badly I could barely keep them open. I saw shadows of animals swoop across the walls and everyone's face looking like melting wax. I could feel myself swaying back and forth, and Sam reached out his arm to steady me.

"What do you see?" he asked, his voice distant and far off, as if he was speaking from a different room.

"Skeletons in the fire," I heard myself say.

"Bones of the Grandfathers," he whispered. "Don't be afraid of them."

By sunrise I was completely exhausted. I was so sick to my stomach, I could barely sit up. But I hadn't vomited like Yvette or the others, and I remember thanking the Creator — my God — for keeping me safe throughout the night.

After Yvette brought in the morning water, and the offerings of dried meat, corn, and berries were served, the meeting was officially over. But there was one more ceremony. Yvette went to her room and brought out various gifts. She gave me some clothes and an eagle feather. She announced that she was adopting me as her son. She said the Creator had spoken to her, had told her to help me on my life's path. My new family hugged me and welcomed me into their circle.

In spite of the apprehension I felt about the meeting, I accepted my new family as if they were my own. They were kind and caring, helpful and wise. They followed traditional ways and they were proud to be Indians. Furthermore, they loved and accepted me.

Family connections have always been important to Native people. In the old days, if a child was orphaned, he or she was taken in by aunties or uncles, grandparents, or even close friends of the child's parents. The child became a full member of that family and the new relationship was never discussed. The same held true for intertribal warfare and the taking of slaves. Slaves often became members of the tribe and were given new names and a new family. In Cree to be without family is to be "*chee-maksow*" (very poor).

The devastating effects of the residential schools and the "scoop" of Native/Métis children from the fifties to seventies, when many were adopted out to white people as far away as Europe, left entire communities robbed and empty. Thousands of children grew up without knowing their roots or families, or that they were even Native. To this day, many of them are still searching for their families and communities, making "*ne-toh-temak*" (relations) along the way. Yvette was trying to heal those scars.

By now I had very little to do with Mom or Aunty. I felt that I no longer needed them. I didn't need Aunty Sandra or the others either. I had always been the black sheep — the odd one. My new family had much more to offer. Finally I had a place to belong, a place without the weight of the past.

I still hadn't told Yvette about Kevin, and I hoped the pain would go away. But it didn't. I wanted so much to confide in her, tell her the truth, but how could I, now that I was her son? What if she was ashamed of me? Besides, I couldn't embarrass her in front of her family.

I continued on with school and finished my grade-eleven course requirements, but I was still too young to write the grade-twelve exam. I had to wait another year until I turned nineteen. Leaving school was difficult. It had been such a rich part of my life. It had kept me focused and occupied. Now there was nothing left to do but collect welfare and wait. But wait for what?

Over the next few months I did nothing but beadwork and craft projects, going to various powwows and gatherings. Like everyone else in the house on welfare, I gave Yvette money for food and rent. I seldom left the house except to visit friends or attend Family Night. I hardly spoke to Mom or Aunty any more, and I couldn't remember the last time I had seen them. My only focus was the family and, as always, the next meeting.

But I still missed Kevin and thought about him every day. Yvette continued to question me, and I came up with every excuse possible to explain my sadness. Then one night she called me into her room. She handed me a picture of Kevin and me that I kept in my wallet. She said that Kyle had found it on the floor. It had been taken in a photo booth a few weeks after we'd met. In the picture we were kissing.

I felt the blood rush to my head.

"Your roommate?" she asked, handing me the picture.

The silence was so heavy I could feel it. "Sort of," I whispered. "I don't want to talk about it."

"Maybe you should," she encouraged. "You seem to be in a lot of pain."

I couldn't even look at her. My mouth was trembling and I couldn't speak.

"Greg, it's okay," she said softly, motioning for me to sit down. "Nothing can be that bad."

I sat down on the edge of the bed and looked at the floor.

"Do you love him?" she asked.

"Yes," I managed. Suddenly tears were streaming down my face and everything came gushing out.

Yvette listened to the entire story, and after I was finished she hugged me and told me that she loved me. I felt such a weight lifted off my shoulders. I even felt better about Kevin. Finally the truth was out — and it wasn't as bad as I thought. She promised not to say anything, and told me if ever I needed to talk, she would always be there.

What do I owe her honour, a life
story that kept her mouth busy?
How easy to impress me, making
relations in a peyote ceremony.
K Mart clothes sealed new blood
ties; ever a sneaky way how she
worked.

Her rush training me to act the
proper son left me thinking we
should be married. She didn't
want to hear my troubles, just my
sex life. I needed to
expose old lovers, put down the
bottle, attend more ceremonies.

She would have done well running
a residential school. The whole
family confessed on themselves.
They sat around gloomy, awaiting
her priestly wisdom. I was too
stubborn. Her ulcer was a good
excuse, blaming me for being too
private.

She wanted to put up an undoing
ceremony. Damn smart move, that
got me talking. Everywhere she
went she spread my dirt. Years

later, seeing her at a powwow,
I pitied her.

I feel outraged when I think back to that time. Trust is important, especially to someone who has had so few people to believe in, yet when used to manipulate and control it can destroy someone permanently. That night I believed Yvette loved and cared about me. I believed that she wanted me to be happy and content within myself. I even believed that she loved me more than my own mother did.

Summer came and I started to dread the meetings. They seemed cultish and they scared me. I honoured the sweatlodge and the things that were brought into the tipi, like the drum, rattle, eagle feathers, and the medicines like the sweetgrass, sage, and cedar. But I didn't honour the peyote. To me, it was a drug and it went against the Creator's laws of living a clean and sober life. Also, I couldn't understand why we had to have a meeting every time there was a problem.

When I tried to tell Yvette how I felt, she refused to listen. She said that I was acting "white" and that I was being disrespectful to Grandfather Peyote. She threatened to throw me out. The family now treated me like an outsider, too. They hardly spoke to me, and I knew that Yvette had told them about Kevin. They watched me like a hawk whenever I was around Kyle, making me feel self-conscious.

I continued to go to meetings, although I hated them. I felt as if I had no choice. It was either that or be kicked out of the house. So I hid my feelings. I even tried to win my place back in the family, but it was too late. The damage was done. I had been careless enough to tell Yvette about Kevin and, worse yet, I'd questioned Grandfather Peyote.

In July, after my nineteenth birthday, Tammy, Sam, Yvette, and I went on a trip to get more peyote. We drove to Arizona and then to Oklahoma. On the way home we stopped in Montana and stayed at the Rocky Boy Reservation. It was the best part of the trip — here I met my own people for the first time. They were Chippewa-Cree and many of them were the descendants of the half-breeds who had fled from Saskatchewan to Montana after the resistance in 1885.

The people in Rocky Boy spoke Cree and followed the traditional ways of the pipe, Sun Dance, and sweatlodge. As soon as they found out I was Cree, they treated me as family. Yvette became cold and wouldn't speak to me, but I didn't care. I was happy to be with my own people, to hear Cree again.

We stayed with an older couple named Rodger and Alice Spotted Horse. Alice was a few years older than Aunty and she even looked like her. She had light brown eyes and a kind face, full of love and humour. Rodger reminded me of a wise grandfather. He was quiet and thoughtful, spiritually involved. He had a sweatlodge and held ceremonies for people on the reservation. But it was Alice that I became close to. She reminded me so much of Aunty.

I confided in her and told her about the meetings and how the family treated me because I didn't believe in Grandfather Peyote. She listened and shook her head in disbelief. After I was finished, she took my hand and said, "My boy, they're not your family. You're a Cree and we have our own sacred ways."

The next day she took me to *Ne-pakwe-chee-mowin* (the Thirsting Dance), which is better known as the Sun Dance.

It was the first time in years that the Sun Dance was being held in Rocky Boy. The grounds overlooked the rolling hills of the reservation, and in the distance stood the skeletons of old lodges. A new lodge had been built and, inside, the dancers bobbed up and down to the steady beat of the drummers. The women wore brightly coloured ribbon skirts and blouses, eagle-bone whistles around their necks, and bands of sage around their head, wrists, and ankles. The men were bare-chested, also wearing long skirts, eagle-bone whistles, and bands of sage. They seemed to be in another world, their bare feet almost lifting off the ground. The smell of sweetgrass and sage hung heavy in the air and the screeching of the dancers' whistles pierced my ears. Outside the lodge, hundreds of people watched the dancers, all of them just as hypnotized as I was.

Alice and I stayed until sunset. The dancers were finished for the day and they would rest until sunrise the following morning. They were to dance another three days, and then the ceremony would be over.

The next day, before we left for home, Alice took me aside while Yvette and Sam packed the van. There were tears in her eyes.

"My boy," she said, "you can stay here as long as you like. I don't feel good about these people."

"I can't," I said, although in my heart I wanted to. "I can't leave Mom and Aunty."

She nodded her head and smiled.

"You're a good boy. Don't let them destroy your spirit. You'll always have a place here with us," she said, pointing to her heart. "Rocky Boy is your home, too, and you're welcome here any time."

She hugged me, and I took from my finger the carved silver ring that Kevin had given me and gave it to her.

"*Kin-na-skomtin Nohkum*" (Thank you, Grandmother), I said, and hugged her again.

As we were pulling out of the driveway, Alice's daughter came rushing out. She handed Sam a shirt, Yvette a fringed dance shawl, and me a beautiful blanket with an eagle on it.

"Mom wants you to have this," she said, catching my eyes for a brief moment.

Yvette was quiet for a long time and then she finally said, "That's a nice gift. The old lady must have really liked you. I wonder why?"

She went back to looking out the window, dismissing me like the rolling hills of Montana behind us.

Eighteen

Land of the Grandfathers

I couldn't believe I was moving back to Maple Ridge with Mom. She had rented a drafty little shack on the outskirts of town, and in spite of its dilapidated condition, I was now grateful to be away from Yvette and the family.

Mom had changed so much that I hardly recognized her. She looked as worn out as the shack — old and beaten down, tired of life, tired of struggling, tired of being alone. Her empty life broke my heart. I felt guilty for the months when I didn't speak to her, for carelessly neglecting her as if she meant nothing at all. I told her about Yvette, the family, and the meetings. I felt that I owed her an explanation, hoping that she would forgive me and realize that I loved her, that I'd always loved her.

Mom tried to encourage me to go back to school, but I just sat in front of the TV, doing beadwork. As long as my hands were busy, I didn't need to think. Finally she gave me an ultimatum: either I stopped feeling sorry for myself and picked myself up, or I had to move out. Though I was angry with her, I knew that she was trying to help me. I half-heartedly looked for work in Vancouver and filled out an application for Native housing. I was certain nothing would come of it, but at least it was a start.

To my amazement, the phone rang a couple of weeks later. My application had been approved and I could move in right away. I fell in love with the suite at once. It was a large, bright bachelor suite in a brand new building in east Vancouver. It had a large kitchen and washroom. The living and dining room was freshly carpeted and in the hallway there were plenty of closets and storage space. The rent was cheap and included utilities.

Mom and I went shopping and bought new dishes, towels, bedding, and whatever else I needed. I picked up some second-hand furniture, and Mom gave me her hide-a-bed couch. I moved in just before the holidays and had everything unpacked and put into its place the same day.

The first night I lay on the living-room floor and looked around the suite. Hanging on the wall behind the couch was the blanket that Alice had given me. Somehow the eagle looked different; it looked free and indomitable, its outstretched wings seeming to lift higher and higher. I thought back to my child-hood, to the many places I'd lived and the many people who had come in and out of my life. I thought about Mom and her strug-gles and how she'd encouraged me to find contentment. I even thought about Kevin, although I felt differently about him now. He seemed powerless, a mere memory that had floated into the past along with the others. Finally I had my own home. No one could hurt me here.

For weeks I couldn't believe my good fortune. I felt that the Creator had blessed me, had somehow reached out and given me another chance. I began using the medicines again, praying with sweetgrass and sage, the *we-ke-mah-kah-sekun* Aunty had given me years ago. I thought about the Sun Dance in Rocky Boy, remembering the power I had felt. I quit drinking and decided to follow the traditional ways.

I sat up late listening to music and doing beadwork. I also began to write again. The poems seemed to come from a new place, almost as if I'd discovered a magical pool of words and feelings, a river that seemed to run through my veins and slip out my fingertips on to the paper. Now I found myself writing about the *power* of being Native, the *power* of the Grandmothers and Grandfathers, even the *power* of my own heart and spirit.

Towards summer I found a job at the Native Counselling and Referral Centre, the same place where Rachel had worked. My job was to assist the alcohol and drug counsellor over the summer and to provide support, housing, and educational information to Native people new to the city. I also visited inmates in jail and people in the hospital or various detox centres. I loved my job and did my utmost to be supportive, just as Rachel had been for me.

Lauren, who also worked at the centre, was two years older, extremely quiet and shy. She was from Hazelton, B.C., and had two children from previous relationships. Because she worked as a hospital liaison worker, we often went to visit the same people. Whenever we worked together, she became excruciatingly shy and timid, even awkward. So I was surprised when a co-worker told me that she was interested in me.

Lauren was the most beautiful woman I'd ever seen. She was petite and fine-featured with fair skin, high cheekbones, long dark hair, and big brown eyes that radiated warmth and compassion. She was gentle and soft-spoken, thoughtful and funny. Like me, she had quit drinking and was interested in learning more about the traditional ways.

By now I had practically forgotten about Kevin and the whole gay scene. I felt as if I had started life over. Only this time I had the choice to be who I wanted. I was normal and straight, determined to get married and have a family like everyone else. Lauren and I began dating, and for the first time I felt entirely good about myself. I met her six-month-old daughter, and soon I was taking them out and spending my days with them. I felt as if I had my very own family, and I couldn't bring myself to tell her anything about the past.

A short time later I met Ryan Peeyaychew, a Cree from North Battleford, Saskatchewan, who was new to Vancouver and was working at the centre as an outreach worker. At twenty-six, he was very accomplished for his age. He had gone through university and had his teaching diploma. He had taken the outreach job only until he could find a teaching position.

I liked Ryan immediately. I remember the first time I met him. He had come over to the drop-in centre for some reason and I mistook him for a client. He laughed and made a joke about looking poor and lost. We started talking and he told me that he was Cree from Saskatchewan. My eyes lit up and I asked him, "*Ke-nay-he-yow-wan?*" (Do you speak Cree?)

"*A-ha*," he said, "*keya-maka?*" (Yes, what about you?)

"*Tapway*" (for sure), I replied, feeling smart and proud.

"*Tanday-ochee-keya?*" (Where are you from?)

"*Ne-mosoom ochee Portage la Prairie*" (My grandfather's from Portage la Prairie). "But," I was quick to add, "he resettled in Prince Albert."

Ryan nodded his head and smiled politely.

"Where did you learn Cree, your *mosoom*?" he asked.

"*Namoya. Ne-ma-sis*" (No. My Aunty).

"Do you speak fluently?"

"Pretty good," I shrugged, trying to be confident. "I can hold my own."

He bit his lip to keep from smiling.

"What do you know?" he asked, looking at me carefully.

I thought for a moment and then lifted my hand to my head and stroked my hair. The only word I could think of was *hair*.

"*Mistuguy!*" I proudly exclaimed.

"*Cha!*" — he frowned — "you're bragging."

"What do you mean?" I was sure that I had said it correctly.

He shook his head and started to laugh.

"You just told me that you have a big penis," he corrected.

I was so embarrassed I wanted to crawl under the desk. He told me the right way to say *hair* and I gladly memorized it. For years after, he called me "*mistuguy*" and often teased me about being such a braggart.

Soon I met his wife, Debbie, and their children, Tonya and Sherman, who were six and five. Debbie was a few years younger than Ryan and came from a reserve not far from where he grew up. It was evident that she loved her family a great deal. She followed Cree customs and was proud of her traditional role as wife and mother. The first time I met her, she gave me a pair of moccasins after supper, saying that she was honoured by my visit.

Ryan came from a large family — ten brothers and four sisters. Most of the younger ones, like Ryan, grew up in foster homes — Native homes — and had been physically and sexually abused. Some of the stories he told me brought tears to my eyes. Even our own people could be neglectful. The older ones had spent time in jail or living on the streets. Some of them had gone to residential school and had suffered equally horrible things.

Ryan was the first of his family to come to Vancouver. Soon after, his brothers followed and they started a powwow drum group called the Red Road Warriors that celebrated sobriety and healing through Native spirituality and culture. Like a lot of Native people I met around that time, the Peeyaychew boys had sobered up and gone back to the sacred ways. Various Native AA groups sprang up around the city and Lauren and I, Ryan and his brothers went to meetings regularly. These meetings were based upon the Twelve Steps and the general principles and philosophies of AA. Before each meeting there was a smudge ceremony. These ceremonies served to purify one's mind and spirit and to cleanse the room of any bad energy. Sweetgrass or sage was burned and the smudge was taken around the room to each person. The smoke was passed over the head and body, almost like bathing with water. Prayers were said and sometimes a song was sung. After the meetings, the boys drummed and sang while everyone visited over coffee and snacks.

I wasn't a stranger to AA, as I had attended meetings with Mom years ago. But these meetings were different. There was a collective awareness, a sense of community in the room. The more I heard the stories of other Native people, the less alone I felt. A common thread ran through our lives. A lot of us had come from alcohol-torn homes and had endured poverty, racism, abuse, shame, fear, and loneliness. Like our grandparents, parents, uncles, and aunties, we had tried to bury the pain with alcohol and drugs, only to find that our lives were a nightmare, a nightmare that had begun generations ago. Only now we were sober and looking to the traditional ways for guidance and healing.

I joined the Red Road Warriors and began to learn various powwow songs, travelling to powwows all across Canada. It's hard to describe the power of the drum: the voices as they rise and fall together; the steady beat, the "heartbeat" of the drum, and the vibration of the drumsticks and bodies moving in unison. Like my writing, I felt so connected to the Grandmothers and Grandfathers, the sacredness of my own spirit. The songs came from the same magical pool: a place that was strong and wilful, untouched by ugliness or pain.

Ryan and I became extremely close over the next few months. We spent a great deal of time together, going for coffee, talking about our lives and dreams. I told him about my new dream; how I wanted to be a singer like Buffy Sainte-Marie and Bruce Cockburn, and how I wanted to write my own songs. I completely forgot about the past, happy now that I'd found a good and spiritual road. Lauren and I continued dating and I seriously thought about settling down and getting married.

Ryan knew nothing about my past, although I told him about Yvette and the meetings which now seemed like a bad dream. I still thought about men once in a while, but I tried not to. It only confused me. And yet, I felt attracted to Ryan, not so much sexually but emotionally. Like me, a part of him seemed to be sad, searching for a place of belonging and some sort of healing. Beneath his humour and teasing laughter there was pain and silence — a silence I could feel. But he also possessed a great deal of strength and determination, something that I'd just become aware of within myself.

Ryan wasn't particularly close to his brothers, not the way we were friends. He adopted me as his *Ne-seem* (little brother), and I happily accepted our new relationship. Oddly enough, we could have truly been half-brothers. We were both tall and slim, with the same strong Cree features and similar mannerisms, only he had black curly hair, dark skin and eyes. People often asked if we were brothers, and I teased him about being the ugly one.

Ryan took a teaching job at Carnegie Centre on East Hastings Street, working with adults, most of whom were heroin addicts and alcoholics. My job at the referral centre was finished and I went on unemployment insurance. I missed working, but I kept busy writing and doing beadwork, going to meetings and spending time with Lauren.

A couple of weeks after starting the job, Ryan announced that he'd accepted a teaching position on a remote reserve up north. I was happy for him, but at the same time felt sad. I had come to rely on him so much: his patient ear and good advice, his knowledge of spiritual things and the Cree language. It didn't dawn on me to go with them until Ryan suggested it.

Although I was happy with my life, I still felt as if I had no *real* place of belonging. I had struggled long and hard to find family — a family that I could relate to, a family that honoured our Indianness and pride. I knew I wasn't ready to begin a family of my own, sensing that I would hurt Lauren in the long run if I stayed.

Lauren, of course, was upset that I was leaving. I vowed that nothing would come between us. I told her that I loved her and promised to come to Vancouver often. We would carry on our relationship, only now it would be long distance. Perhaps one day we would get married and she would come to live up north.

After all, Hazelton, her hometown, was only an hour away from where we were going.

We moved at the end of September, all of our belongings packed and the five of us crammed in the front seat of the U-haul. The trip took two days and we camped along the way. At some point, I realized what I had done. I felt guilty for leaving Mom again, for leaving Aunty and Grandma, and now Lauren. I was sorry to leave my beautiful apartment and my friends. Maybe the pattern of moving on was just too deep in me.

Kitwancool, our destination, was between Terrace and Smithers. I had been to Smithers before with Mom and Don, to visit Sherry, but I hadn't been any farther. The Trans-Canada Highway seemed to go on forever, and the surrounding wilderness and marshy valleys were so lush and green I felt as if I'd stepped into an Emily Carr painting. Finally we arrived at Kitwanga, a small town populated mostly by white people. It was a typical small northern town. Out on the highway was the Husky gas station and restaurant. Across the bridge was the reserve and beyond that the town itself, which had a high school, post office, and IGA grocery store. The houses in town were well maintained while the reserve houses looked old and shabby, barely livable. Kitwancool was fifteen miles away and I remember feeling relieved as we pulled out of the reserve.

We arrived just as the sun was sinking into the endless acres of cedar, fir, and spruce. We circled the dirt roads of the reserve, trying to find the band office. Like Kitwanga, the houses looked old and neglected; the curtainless windows revealed the unobtrusive stares of the occupants inside. Some of the houses had been abandoned and left to the elements, while others were in various states of dilapidation. Broken-down cars sat rusting in the yards, most of them stripped for parts. Dogs ran back and forth, baring their teeth and barking. I felt as if I'd entered an alien world.

After we found the band office and Ryan went inside to

announce our arrival, Debbie, the kids, and I waited in the truck, speechless. The strangest feeling came over me. I felt light-headed and dizzy, almost nauseous. Looking out, I saw the totem poles in front of the band office. They were withered and old, oddly familiar. The carved figures seemed to stare into my soul, speaking a language that I faintly remembered. I suddenly recognized the feeling. It was my childhood dream. Grandfather Black Bear!

At that very moment, I knew the Creator had brought me here. Why, I didn't know. But I sensed a power around me. I felt scared and uncertain, just as I had in my dream. And yet I felt protected and light, as if I were about to fly.

Nineteen

Quest into Darkness

The village was even more remote than I had imagined, populated by three hundred people at the most. The ghosts of the dead seemed to whisper from the weed-filled cemetery, drifting freely about the reserve as if the weathered crosses and carved headstones, the cast-iron gates surrounding the graves were meant only to keep intruders out.

There was a sad-looking A-frame Pentecostal church, which had once been painted red and was now in desperate need of repair. The white minister, his wife and young children lived next door in an equally sad-looking trailer. The congregation varied depending upon the season. Few people came to church in the summer as they were busy fishing in the Nass Valley. More people, mostly the older ones, attended church in the winter, there being little else to do.

A large, fairly new house served as the band office. Inside were the offices of the chief and his council, the alcohol and drug worker, the secretarial staff, and the social worker, who distributed the monthly welfare payments. In the middle of the village was the large old community hall. The white paint had peeled and chipped and some of the windows were broken and covered over with plastic or cardboard. In spite of its condition, it was still used for weddings, funerals, feasts, and potlatches.

The school, which was the newest building on the reserve, went from kindergarten to grade twelve. Most of the teachers, except Ryan and another teacher from the community, were white and had come from places like Manitoba and Ontario. Many of them stayed only a year and then moved on. They seldom, if ever, had anything to do with the community and spent as little time there as possible. In the baseball field next to the school, the broken-down bleachers and dugout stood eerily empty, looking forsaken amidst the field of potholes and over-grown weeds. There were two houses in the village where you could buy candy, pop, chips, and cigarettes, play arcade games, or rent videos. Also, there were a couple of bootleggers who sold cases of beer or the occasional bottle of hard liquor for a shameless price. It was not at all what I had expected.

Our new home was a small duplex close to the community hall. It had two upstairs bedrooms, a medium-sized kitchen, living room, and washroom. Downstairs there was another bedroom and a small uncarpeted rec-room with cement floors. Beside us lived a stern-looking and unfriendly teacher from Ontario who was in her mid-fifties. She barely spoke to us and we seldom saw her, as she left on the weekends.

The community had little to do with us until they got to know Ryan. He taught grade ten, and in no time his students were coming over to the house. Word quickly spread that we didn't drink and we followed traditional ways. Soon everyone began to drop in. We were the first sober family to live there and they were interested in our "prairie ways."

Debbie and I became extremely close. The people my age already had close friends, which made me feel even more like an outsider. I was shy and nervous around them, convinced they would see me as weird. Debbie felt like an outsider, too. On days when I was depressed, I would talk to her and she would make me laugh; and I would do the same for her when needed.

I missed Vancouver, the size and freedom of the city. I missed the cafés and clothing stores. I missed the parks and beaches, even the constant blaring of horns and sirens. I missed Davie Street and, in spite of the shame and guilt I felt, the cruising glances of attractive men. I missed my apartment where I was able to lock the world out when I wanted. I missed Lauren and my friends from AA. I wanted it all back, but now it was too late.

Besides helping Debbie with the household chores and kids, I wrote, did beadwork, went for long walks, and slept a great deal. Although I sensed the Creator had brought me here, I hated myself for so thoughtlessly leaving everything behind. I could feel myself growing more and more impatient by the day, waiting for a sign — any sign — to show me my life's purpose.

The leaves began to change colour and fall from the trees. Winter hung heavy in the air and the days grew dark and cold. Except for the occasional trip to Kitwanga or Terrace (a real town with cafés and shopping malls), I had little else to look forward to. I wrote long letters to Mom and Grandma, to Aunty, Lauren, and my friends. I called Lauren every week and begged her to move up north.

By now I was back on welfare. Ryan and I drifted apart and our closeness was gone. I secretly blamed him for my unhappiness, although I knew it had nothing to do with him. I was responsible for leaving Vancouver, responsible for the unhappiness I felt. My desire for family, a place of belonging, had outweighed everything. And now I was paying the price. Debbie was just as unhappy, but for different reasons. She and Ryan barely spoke, and the tension between them seemed to get worse.

A short time later Ryan got me a job teaching drama, and I enthusiastically prepared some sort of course outline. I pored over old worksheets I'd saved from Spirit-Song. I dug out my books on acting and various plays like George Ryga's *Ecstasy of Rita Joe* and Shakespeare. Finally I had something worthwhile to do, and I was determined to make it a success.

My first class was held at the community hall. I had twelve students, most of whom were Ryan's, and I handed them the course outline. Bursting with excitement, I looked around the huge hall, eyeing the stage, and imagined the entire community turning out to see *Rita Joe*. But there was a lot of preparation needed. There were warm-up exercises and voice lessons, just as I had learned at Spirit-Song. Before the end of the class most of the students politely excused themselves. Although they didn't say anything, I knew what they were thinking. Stretching and making weird noises had nothing to do with with *real acting*.

I went home and tried not to be discouraged. I knew my approach must seem crazy, especially to a bunch of kids who'd never been to the city, let alone been involved with the arts. I convinced myself the next class would be better and they wouldn't be so shy. But the following week I stood alone, worksheets and a copy of *Rita Joe* in my hands. The hall looked as empty as I felt. No one had even bothered to say they weren't coming.

Debbie and Ryan never discussed their troubles in front of me. But over time, Debbie confided in me. She accused Ryan of being a womanizer, saying that he'd had numerous affairs and didn't want to be married, at least not to her. She cried and told me that she loved him and wanted things to work out. Because Ryan was my brother (by now I had taken the Peeyaychew name as my own father's name meant nothing to me), I tried not to take sides. But Debbie and I were also close and I felt I owed her my support. I found myself caught in the middle. I loved both of them, and I understood their frustration and pain.

I knew that I was feeling sorry for myself and decided that Ryan was right about my attitude. He had said that I was acting like a "spruce among the poplar" — that everyone in the village thought I was a snob and that I should try to be a bit more friendly. So over the next few weeks I made an effort to meet people and make friends. I hung out with people my own age and we played cards, listened to music, watched videos, and drove aimlessly around the reserve. But no matter how hard I tried, I couldn't relate to them. Most of them liked to party, and because I didn't drink, I felt out of place.

After several months I knew everyone in the village and had made friends with a few older people, most of whom were married with kids. But I was back to drinking again. Everyone drank, and at some point I just gave in. It seemed a lot easier to be like everyone else and forget about the future.

Ryan and Debbie decided to separate, but then Debbie discovered she was three months' pregnant. Ryan refused to believe the baby was his, and accused her of having an affair. He told her that she could stay until the baby was born, but then she had to leave. Our lives were breaking apart. Ryan threw himself into teaching and Debbie took a cleaning job at the band office. Meanwhile, I drank all night with my friends, staggering home at six or seven in the morning.

Now Ryan and I argued constantly and I tried my best to avoid him. Even Debbie and I drifted apart. She seemed to be in a world of her own, as if she was a prisoner awaiting her execution.

I had nothing to look forward to except my welfare cheque and driving into Terrace to shop, eat, and drink. We sat in the bars until closing time, getting so drunk that we could barely walk. It was a miracle that we never got into a car accident. It was 150 miles back to the reserve on roads covered with black ice and snowdrifts.

And yet as drunk as I got, I remember feeling ashamed of myself. I had been proud of my sobriety, of following the Red Road. Now, in the back of mind, I could hear the taunting remarks of the white kids I'd gone to school with — the cruel things they'd said about drunken Indians and reserves. I felt completely disgusted with myself for becoming one of their stereotypical jokes.

Yet a part of me still sensed the Creator had brought me here. Not long after we came to the reserve I began to have a recurring dream that my hair was long, almost down to my waist. I would brush it out, rub bear grease into it, braid it, and tie the ends with white buckskin. In other dreams I would be at a powwow, braiding my hair in a tent or tipi, frantically trying to hurry because Grand Entry, when all of the dancers enter the arbour before the powwow officially begins, was starting.

These dreams briefly filled me with an incredible sense of pride. I felt connected to the Grandmothers and Grandfathers, to the ancient warriors whose blood ran through my veins. Yet the dreams, no matter how strong they made me feel at the time, seemed just as puzzling as did my long-ago dream of Grandfather Black Bear.

I had started a dancing outfit for myself shortly after coming to Kitwancool. The beadwork was the most beautiful I'd ever done — geometric designs in white, black, two shades of red, and silver. The moccasins were fully beaded and I had made a matching belt, bandolier, headpiece, breastplate, and cuffs. I had spent countless hours sewing after everyone went to bed, listening to powwow music, imagining myself dancing strong and hard into the arbour for Grand Entry. I had even imagined myself with long, beautiful braids trailing down my chest.

By now, my project sat in the corner collecting dust. I knew that as long as I was drinking, I couldn't dance. I had enough respect for the Creator that I didn't dare touch the medicines or anything sacred, not even the little *Twenty-four Hours a Day* book that Mom had given me. It was filled with AA meditations and prayers, and I had read it religiously every morning before getting out of bed. On the inside cover she had inscribed, "Dear Greg, always keep this near. I promise you that you can get through absolutely anything. Read it every morning when it's peaceful and quiet. I love you, Mom."

Besides losing my sobriety, I felt great shame at something that had happened a few weeks back. Someone had killed a black bear and I helped to skin it. It was night-time and the bear was sprawled out on its back, its eyes wide and glassy looking in the glow of the floodlight. I wanted the claws for my outfit and I struggled for hours to cut them off. Everyone had gone inside and I was alone with the dead bear. I began to feel sick to my stomach, but I was determined to get the claws. Up to this point, I hadn't even thought about my sacred dream. But then it suddenly hit me. I felt like *We-te-koow*, the cannibal. Here I was butchering the spirit-keeper who had given me medicine and told me I had much work to do. I fell to my knees and silently prayed, *Grandfather, forgive me for what I've done.* But the medicine was gone — I could feel it in my heart. In its place was emptiness.

Debbie left after the holidays to visit her family in Saskatchewan. The baby was almost due and she wanted to make preparations to move home. I was angry with Ryan for his indifferent attitude towards her, disgusted by his heartlessness. But I kept my thoughts to myself, hoping things would somehow work out for them.

Debbie's water broke on the train coming home, and she was rushed to the hospital in Prince George. A week later she arrived back with a beautiful baby boy, whom she'd named Ian Gregory, after her late brother and myself. Ryan seemed happy and proud. He held a special ceremony for the baby and asked me to be the godfather. But in spite of everything, he still asked Debbie to leave. She silently packed her clothes and left a few days later with Tonya and the baby. Sherman remained with Ryan. She left me her mother's phone number and made me promise to call.

I knew Ryan was getting close to kicking me out, too, and I didn't want to make trouble. But I was angry with myself for becoming a reserve drunk, for feeling sorry for myself and giving up on life. I hadn't spoken or written to Mom, Aunty, or Lauren in months. Furthermore, I hadn't written a single poem or story. I decided to sober up again, and asked the Creator to help me.

One weekend the phone rang at two o'clock in the morning. My friends wanted me to come over and party with them, but I said no. A few minutes later, the phone rang again. It was another friend who needed my help to take her niece, Clara, home. She was drunk, smashing things, and trying to fight with people.

I found Clara, calmed her down and took her home. She was so drunk she couldn't even stand up. I had to practically drag her through the snow. She was the same age as I was and she, too, wanted to be a writer. We had talked hundreds of times about poetry and writing, had read poems to one another, and she dreamed about going to university down south.

The entire reserve seemed to be drunk that night. People were driving around in the cars, yelling and throwing beer bottles at the street lights. Some people were fighting, and I could hear children crying. By the time I got home, Ryan was still awake and I went to his room to talk.

"You get Clara home okay?" he asked.

"Yeah," I sighed, "but I don't need to watch a western on TV where all the Indians are getting mowed down by the cavalry."

"What do you mean?" he frowned.

"It's a nightmare out there" — I shook my head — "no one gives a shit about anything."

He sat up in bed, momentarily puzzled. His eyes grew wide and his voice took on an indignant tone.

"I recall," he began, "just last week you were staggering home at six in the morning. What gives you the right to judge?"

"Well, I've got dreams!" I shouted.

"And that makes you somehow better!" he shouted back.

"No! But I'd never raise my kids on a reserve."

"What the fuck do you know about reserves!" he yelled. "You never grew up on one!"

I went to say something, but before I knew it, he was out of bed and had pressed me up against the closet doors. It was such a shock, it took me a minute to feel anything. I braced myself for the same thing I'd grown up with all my life. But Ryan didn't hit me. He got back into bed and I left his room, trembling from head to toe.

In that moment his anger took me right back to the power-lessness of my childhood. Suddenly I hated him as much as I hated Don and Uncle Tim. I made up my mind to leave. I saw clearly that my life consisted of leaving people I loved. But I also saw that I was an adult now, a capable and strong-willed individual who had only himself to blame for his unhappiness.

I called Debbie the next day and made arrangements to come to Saskatchewan. I didn't want to go back to Vancouver — I felt there was nothing there for me. I had already lost touch with everyone — even Mom. I had failed at everything: my sobriety, my writing and singing dreams. Kitwancool, like my long-ago vision of Grandfather Black Bear, felt like another hopeless attempt at finding my spirit. Maybe things would be better in a new place. Maybe this time I would find happiness, if *I* allowed it.

Twenty

Pekewe, Pekewe (Come Home, Come Home)

In March of 1986, one week after I called Debbie, I sat on the station platform in Hazelton, all of my clothes and belongings packed in a suitcase, waiting for the train to Saskatoon. Although I was twenty, I felt as if I was a ten-year-old again. The melting clumps of snow held the promise of spring and new beginnings, which in any other time would have filled me with a childlike hope, even excitement.

The train chugged across B.C. and through the snow-capped Rockies, past Alberta and finally into Saskatchewan. I was awestruck by the flatness of the land, the wide open sky, and the hills that seemed to roll on without end, the sleepy-looking grain elevators that bore the names of towns, the old farmhouses, and endless acres of still-frozen wheat disappearing in the blink of an eye. I didn't miss the mountains as I had thought, but instead felt a sense of freedom and openness, a strange comfort at leaving the coast behind. Years later, I would write a poem capturing my return to my roots.

> *In Saskatoon*
> *I escaped to the lumpy bed*
> *my nitim's cousin provided.*
> *Her old man*

was in jail
so it was okay.
At the Albany Hotel
I learned
busted lips were from
not sitting stiff
with my back to the wall.
My first black-out
I was a tranquilized bear
dumped
somewhere between 20th Street
and the railroad tracks.

That bear claw necklace
hung above my bed
reminding me of my cannibal sins
until the day
I sold it.

---

nitim: sister-in-law

I stayed with Debbie's cousin for a week, but then had to leave because her boyfriend was getting out of jail. Debbie made arrangements for me to stay with another cousin who lived closer to downtown. I had twenty-five dollars to my name and I searched high and low for a job, but finding work was impossible — either I didn't have enough education or lacked experience.

It didn't take me long to realize that Saskatoon, like most other prairie towns and cities, was highly racist. Although I wasn't visibly Native, many prospective employers would see my last name (Peeyaychew) and, without even looking at me, say, "Sorry, but the job is filled."

By now, as I was out of money and had no prospects of work, I went to welfare and made an appointment to see a worker. I had to wait two weeks and in the meantime I continued to look for a job. Finally the day of my appointment came and I crossed my fingers that I would get some help. I sat in the welfare office for three hours before the worker saw me. She finally called my name and I followed her to her office. I sat there with my head down while she read my application. She didn't even look at me.

"Why are you coming here instead of Indian Affairs?" she asked.

"I'm not status," I mumbled.

"But it says here you were collecting social assistance on a reserve in British Columbia."

"I don't have status," I repeated.

She looked up from the form and gave me an icy look.

"Then what are you?" she asked indignantly.

"Half-breed," I whispered, unsure whether or not I had actually said it.

"Then why were you getting welfare on an Indian reserve?"

"I don't know," I shrugged.

I was so humiliated I wanted to bolt out of her office. The worker chewed her bottom lip for a moment before she continued.

"I don't know if I can help you. You're not a resident of Saskatchewan — you're not a treaty Indian — besides, you should have just stayed on the reserve."

"But there was no work there — I don't know why — I just wanted to leave and come here," I stammered.

She shrugged her shoulders and shook her head.

"I'm sorry but I can't do anything. Maybe I can get you a bus ticket back to Kitwancool or whatever it's called."

A bus ticket! I was trying so hard to be patient and calm. My head felt as if it was going to explode.

"But I don't have any food," I argued. "I can't live off the people I'm staying with."

"Maybe you should have thought about that before coming

here," she reproached. She shrugged her shoulders again and started to say something but I cut her off.

"I don't want a God damn bus ticket!" I shouted. "And I don't need your fucking help! Shove it!"

I marched out of her office, wondering what I would do now.

The next few weeks were desperate. I borrowed some money from Debbie, and after that was gone I crawled back to welfare and was given a food voucher. Finally I had no choice but to pawn my leather jacket, Walkman, and tapes. I took what little money I got and bought some food, beads, and scrap leather. I sewed night and day, everything from key chains to baby moccasins until I had enough things to sell. I bought more supplies and continued to sell my work. Sometimes I went from sewing to the casual labour office at six o'clock in the morning. Occasionally I was lucky and would get an odd job, mostly gardening or painting. Either way the jobs were a godsend — it was money.

Things looked so dismal I decided to go back to school. Welfare agreed to help me, providing I attended school full-time. I still didn't have my grade twelve, and it was clear no one would hire me until I got it. The community college had upgrading courses for adults, similar to the Native Education Centre, and I hoped to complete grade twelve in a couple of months. But I did miserably on the entrance exam, especially in math. I wrote the exam twice and failed.

I couldn't keep sponging off Debbie's cousin, buying groceries whenever I got money. She was on welfare and could barely afford to feed herself and her daughter. I was sure that I would end up on the street or in a men's hostel, until the day I met Alana Daystar, a guidance counsellor who worked at the college.

Alana was one of those rare people the Creator sets on your path when everything seems hopeless. I met her the second time I failed the exam. I was about to leave when one of the instructors took me to see her. I walked into her office, sat down, and started to cry.

"I'm sorry," I sobbed into my hands, "but I don't know what to do any more."

She pulled her chair beside mine, took hold of my hands and gave me a tender look.

"Hey, it's okay," she smiled. "I feel like that a lot of the time."

I took a deep breath and tried not to let my voice tremble.

"I failed the exam — twice!" I admitted. "And if I don't get into school, welfare won't help me."

"Don't worry," she frowned. "I'll call them and say you've written the exam."

I looked at her optimistically, unsure whether or not she had heard me.

"But I failed!"

"Yeah, so big deal," she shrugged. "It's only a test. Next time you'll do better."

Her gentle assurance was like a mother's embrace. For the first time I saw the woman sitting across from me. She was in her mid-forties, short and slender, with dark eyes that radiated warmth and compassion. Her thick black hair was twisted into a bun and fastened with a large beaded barrette. She wore a silver bracelet and miniature feather earrings, a T-shirt with a Native logo, jeans, and Birkenstock sandals.

I felt great peace in my heart, and knew it was the Creator's plan for me to meet her. We talked for hours and I told her everything. Her kind, no-nonsense attitude filled me with hope, and by the time I left her office I wondered if I would ever know the kind of quiet strength she seemed to possess.

> One lousy food voucher
> held up the line,
> my worker's generosity
> was the half-empty bag
> I lugged home.
> Outside the music store

hot tears
drenched my Opry dream
and scorched
my throat permanently.
My first poem
was a stub pencil
scrawling notes
on brown paper.

    *

At the community college
downtown
she was the brown face
I confided in.
She talked
distantly of being
slapped at the residential school
how
for years after
she wandered homeless
in her bones.

My twenty-first birthday
she took me for dinner
and planted
a garden in my heart.

The following Friday
she dropped by, told me
to pack some things.
"Kiya kak-wechee-ke-maw," she said,
"sew-skwatch itoota."
We drove north past Duck Lake
barely talking

then she simply whispered,
"Greg, pekewe."

"Kiya kak-wechee-ke-maw": Don't ask
"sew-skwatch itoota": just do it
pekewe: come home

When I think back to that time I realize how tired I was of strug-gling, searching for a place of safety and belonging. My past seemed to belong to someone else and my future to a complete stranger. When I looked in the mirror I saw an empty shell — someone without dreams. Many nights I lay in bed and remem-bered Mom's words, "God's gift to you is your life — what you make of it is your gift to God," but they were too painful to think about.

Ryan and Sherman came home in June, after the school year was finished. Debbie told Ryan where to find me, and he came to see me late one evening. As usual, I was doing beadwork, trying to make enough things to sell. He walked into the kitchen, cheerful as if nothing ever happened between us. *"Tansay, Ne-seem?"* (How are you, little brother?) he asked.

I barely looked at him and shrugged my shoulders. "Okay, I guess." He sat down and offered me a smoke. He was silent for a moment and then he frowned.

"Debbie says she hardly ever sees you."

"I've been busy," I said. "Gotta survive somehow."

He looked around the table, silently taking inventory of my work.

"What kind of prices do you get?"

"Enough to get drunk!" I replied drily.

He chewed his bottom lip and nodded. His eyes looked much darker than I remembered.

"How much money do you need?" He dug out his wallet.

"Muk-ke-kway!" (Nothing) I snapped. "I can manage by myself."

A heavy silence stood between us and then he smiled. He shook his head and sighed, "Still as stubborn as ever."

We went for a drive and Ryan spent a couple of hours talking to me. He told me that he was proud of me but that my spirit was wandering and that I needed to look within myself to find it. As I was getting out of his truck he slipped twenty dollars into my hand and said, "Make sure you eat."

Seeing my big brother again affected me deeply. His words rang true somewhere within me.

Ryan went back to Kitwancool a few weeks later and I moved in with a friend of Debbie's cousin. By this time, thanks to Alana, I was getting welfare and was able to pay room and board. I still drank, but I slowed down a lot. I was scared because I'd already had two blackouts and couldn't remember anything. The first time I woke up by the railway tracks, and the second time I woke up on the floor in someone's living room with blood all over my jacket. I had been in the middle of a fight.

I began to seriously think about my life — I would be twenty-one in a couple of days — and I knew I was becoming more and more like Uncle Tim, even Mom. I had sold everything of value, including the beautiful outfit I'd dreamed of wearing. I had given away my pride — my medicine — and everything that I held sacred.

I hadn't seen Alana in quite a while and desperately needed to talk to her. I felt guilty as I walked into her office, but she greeted me with her warm smile. She gave me a big hug and tousled my hair.

"How's my beadworker?" she asked, proudly pointing to the barrettes I had made her.

"Surviving," I sighed, "but that's about all."

A smile broke across her round, dark face. "Well, you're not alone. Believe me, a dozen people come into my office every day who are barely able to make ends meet. Besides, you're young and it comes with the territory. Be patient. The Creator will show you the right path."

"When did you find your path?"

"Over many years — many years of pain and suffering." Her eyes trailed out the window. "Son, I'm a lot older than you," she said, "but we've experienced some of the same things."

I followed her gaze out the window, as if she was about to show me something of great importance.

"I grew up with my grandparents, who were very traditional people, and when I was five I was taken to a residential school near Regina. I didn't speak a word of English — only Cree and Saulteaux — and I was beaten for it." She looked at me and there were tears in her eyes.

"By the time I got out of school," she continued, "I'd completely forgotten the language. I couldn't even remember my grandparents or the things they'd taught me. I went back to the reserve, but everything had changed. My grandparents were dead and I hardly recognized my aunties and uncles."

She wiped her eyes and continued, "I spent a long time trying to find myself, moving from one place to the next. I tried to get rid of the pain by drinking, but it always came back. I felt dead inside and nothing mattered, not even my life."

She got up and went to the window. Her back was to me and she stood there silently looking out on to the street.

"Greg, life is what we make it. The Creator has a special plan for each of us. Sometimes we learn the hard way, but in the end it makes us stronger. Sometimes we have to lose," she hesitated, "in order to appreciate the Creator's gifts."

She went to her desk, pulled open the top drawer, and handed me a braid of sweetgrass.

"Take it," she said and smiled. "I got it from the Sun Dance." I held it in my hands.

My birthday came, but I felt so old I couldn't imagine what it would be like to be a *real* twenty-one-year-old. But Alana insisted that I shouldn't let the day slip by without celebrating. She took me out for supper and later on I called Mom. Hearing her voice made me homesick. I wanted to tell her everything, apologize for leaving, but I couldn't.

It was difficult to accept responsibility for my own actions. I had spent so many years reacting to how other people treated me. It seems odd to me now that I felt so disconnected from myself and the Creator. I knew about the medicines and following the Red Road. It had helped me in the past — had sustained and given me a sense of belonging — but I had chosen to follow a different road, a dead-end road that led to more pain and suffering. I no longer felt connected to anything Native. I felt caught between two worlds and there was no place for me in either.

A week after my birthday, one Friday afternoon, Alana unexpectedly came by the apartment. She told me to pack some things, saying that she was going out of town for the weekend. I asked to where, but she said it was a surprise, and so I went along.

We drove to Prince Albert and stayed overnight with her cousin and his family. The next day, instead of coming home, we stopped in Duck Lake.

"Where are we going?" I asked, mildly irritated that I didn't know the plan.

"Never mind," she frowned. "It's a surprise."

I slumped back in my seat and gazed out at the sunburnt wheat fields, brooding as we passed the old weathered buildings that seemed to sink into the landscape. The powder-blue sky looked endless and open and the clouds seemed to just hang there, swollen and motionless. We drove a little farther and then came to a bridge that crossed the South Saskatchewan River. The scrub poplar and wolf willow leaned against the muddy banks, swaying in the late afternoon breeze.

No sooner had we crossed the bridge than we came to the

gates of a fairground. Above the gates stood a sign which read *Back to Batoche Days*. I looked at Alana for a moment, stunned, and then realized where I was. Suddenly I could hear my school-teachers reading from those history books, talking about crazy Louis Riel and the useless half-breeds. *How could she bring me here?*

"Some surprise!" — I glared at her — "Why didn't you tell me?"

"Because I knew you wouldn't come."

I sighed. I knew she was right.

"Greg, *pekewe*," she said. "It's time you came home."

Home! It was the last place in the world I would ever consider home. I wanted to leave, but Alana said no. She pointed to the highway and told me to hitch-hike if I was so determined to go. I grudgingly helped her pitch the tent. We ate supper in silence and then went to bed. I lay there for a long time, wondering why she had brought me here. If she really cared about me — or so I thought — she would have taken me to a powwow or Sun Dance.

By now it was dark, and in the distance I could hear fiddle music. Alana was asleep and I stepped out of the tent and went to the big top. I sat in the shadows and watched the people visit and dance. They were strangers to me. They weren't like Indians or white people. They were loud and rowdy, full of jokes and gaiety. They laughed, danced, and sang as if nothing else mattered. I thought about Aunty and wished she was with me. Suddenly I needed her guidance and approval. If these were my people, I needed her to say so.

The following afternoon Alana and I sat in the big top and watched the fiddling and jigging competitions. There were fiddlers from Alberta, Saskatchewan, and Manitoba, even as far away as the Northwest Territories. They played traditional Métis music like the "Red River Jig." Many of the reels, jigs, and waltzes had been handed down over the generations. The "jiggers" or "cloggers" were dressed in ribbon shirts and brightly coloured sashes and wore moccasins, dress shoes, or cowboy boots that seemed to glide across the dance floor. Their steps were vigorous and intricate, much like a heel-toe shuffle with various changes. Their steps were in perfect time to the fiddle and were met with thunderous applause. Alana told me the steps were a combination of Indian dancing and Scottish-Irish jigs.

In spite of my indifference, I found myself looking around the crowded big top, intrigued by the people. Some of them were dark and looked distinctly Native while others were fair, with light hair and eyes. I felt oddly attracted to these people. It was evident they were Native, at least to me, but they could easily be mistaken as white. Once again, I thought about Aunty, Mom, too, and I could see them sitting in the bleachers, tapping their toes and clapping their hands.

Afterwards, Alana and I joined the pilgrimage to the mass grave site of the Métis soldiers who were killed in the rebellion. Later, we toured the historical site at Batoche. Only the rectory and chapel remained. The chapel had bullet holes in the walls, and I remember feeling angry and sad for the women and children who sheltered there during the fighting. The Métis homes had long since been looted and burned to the ground by the Canadian troops.

Besides the artifacts and life-size displays of Métis life and the rebellion itself, there was a theatre which had a special show about the Northwest Rebellion. The show was narrated by Gabriel Dumont's character (the military leader of the Métis at Batoche) and told of the struggles leading up to the resistance. It was so unlike anything I had learned at school. The half-breeds, under the guidance of Louis Riel, had petitioned the Macdonald government, wanting assurance of the right to keep the lands on which they'd lived for years, but their requests were repeatedly ignored. Without recourse, Riel established a provisional government, as he'd done in 1869 at Fort Garry in Manitoba, and he instructed the RCMP at Fort Carlton to surrender or the half-breeds would attack.

The RCMP refused. The Battle of Duck Lake took place in March 1885, and was a victory for the Métis. But within a month, close to five thousand troops and RCMP arrived at Batoche, with a gatling gun, and crushed the resistance — 150 Métis soldiers, most of whom were old men, and who were reduced to using small stones and nails for ammunition.

Gabriel Dumont, along with a few of the leaders, escaped to Montana. He eventually returned to Batoche, after years of exile, and died in 1906. Louis Riel surrendered three days after the resistance, in the hope that he could legitimize the Métis cause. However, he was hanged for high treason on November 16, 1885. The history books say that he was crazy, a lunatic who believed he was a prophet, mostly because his legal counsel attempted to prove him innocent by reason of insanity. The people of Batoche scattered to the United States, Alberta, and other Métis communities in Saskatchewan.

By the end of the show, tears were streaming down my face. I felt such a mixture of emotion. A surprising new feeling had awoken within me. I looked around the theatre and saw *my* people. I knew I had come home at last. I reached over and took Alana's hand. All I could manage to say was, "Thank you."

As we left Batoche I felt my heart sink into the very landscape, my spirit joining those of my ancestors in the empty ravines and coulees. I had searched so long for a place of belonging, and now I had found it. The importance that I had once placed on being Cree — a true and pure Indian — seemed to disappear with the sinking sun. Suddenly the colour of my eyes, hair, and skin seemed to *belong* to me, perfectly matching the prairie landscape that held such a dignified history. Now I had new heroes — Louis Riel and Gabriel Dumont, the half-breed soldiers who had given their lives for *our* homeland, freedom and independence. Never again would I search for a place of belonging. This place, Batoche, would always be "home," my home.

In the weeks following the visit to Batoche my life began to change completely. I was accepted as a mature student at the Gabriel Dumont Institute, into the Native Human Justice Program. School was beginning in September and I made arrangements to move to Prince Albert, the same town where my grandparents had lived. More and more I felt a connection with my grandfather, remembering the numerous stories Mom had told me about him. I would walk the same streets and visit the same cafés, only I would hold my head high, proud of the blood thundering through my veins.

A few months ago I went home, back to Saskatchewan to visit family and friends. I hadn't seen Alana in eleven years, and I found her through a mutual friend. We talked for hours and tried to catch up on everything in one afternoon. I gave her a copy of *Native Canadiana: Songs from the Urban Rez* and read her the poem I had written about her. She had tears in her eyes, and when I finished, she said, "Greg, I always knew that you would make it."

She told me about finding her daughter, whom she'd given up for adoption years ago (I didn't know this until now). She said that finding her girl had changed her life, that the Creator had given her a great gift. I looked in her eyes, the same eyes that had given me so much, and I knew in my heart the Creator had only given back to her what she'd given to others. The circle was complete.

> *In the middle of the prairie*
> *I sat*
> *tearing my Cheechum's lodge*
> *screeching*
> *at 101 years of defeat*

to the indigo sky
tasting
the salty blood
of buffalo, rabbit and gopher
than ran ancient
through my veins and
gave life
to our history, the fiddle
as it waltzed
through the empty coulees
at Batoche.

Ekospe-ka-tipskak
the first seed
sprouted
then another and another
until my flesh, my bones
were as rooted
as the sweetgrass
swaying
as far as
the eye could see.

Cheechum: Great-grandmother
Ekospe-ka-tipskak: that night

Twenty-One

A Voice to Speak With

It's hard to capture the many profound changes of that time. The future lay before me, and yet I felt connected to the past, to the things that I had tried so hard to bury. I had never told anyone, even Alana, the exact details of my childhood and wanted to believe the pain would just go away. For as long as I could remember I had always wanted to be someone else and belong to someone else's family.

I enthusiastically began school, feeling that I'd found my life's purpose in human justice. The program was namely for mixed-blood students, most of whom were adults, and concentrated on social work, the criminal justice system, English, correctional training, and Métis history. There were students from various Métis communities like Buffalo Narrows, Ile à La Crosse, Cumberland House, La Ronge, Meadow Lake, and Canoe Lake.

Over the next few months I became friends with a few of my classmates. The old feeling of being different, of not quite fitting in, was gone. I felt strong and proud. We all shared a similar history — many of us coming from families that had kept their heritage a secret.

I spent hours in the school library, reading everything I could get my hands on about Métis culture, and I began to understand why our history was forgotten. We were neither Indians nor white people. Instead, we were a combination of the two, a unique mixture that had produced our own language (Michif), dances and songs, artwork and stories. Our Cree relations called us *Awp-pee-tow-koosons* (Half-sons) and, for the most, considered us white. The whites refused to accept us altogether, believing we were Indians or "dirty breeds." However, we called ourselves *Bois brulé* (Burnt-wood People), half-breeds, Métis, mixed-bloods, or *Ka-tip-aim-soo-chick* (The People Who Own Themselves).

The more I read, the more I began to understand why my grandfather, like so many others, had chosen to deny the truth. For their generation, being Métis meant a life of hopelessness, racism, and deprivation. Just as I had denied the truth and *wanted* to be all Cree, to have a place of belonging, so had my grandfather. I remember my grandmother telling me about their meeting, and how after they decided to marry, his brother had commented, "What in the hell does she possibly see in you!"

I received a small living allowance for school but found it almost impossible to survive. By the time I paid the rent and phone bill, there was hardly enough money left to buy groceries. Thankfully, my landlady, an older woman who belonged to the Legion, brought me leftovers from their get-togethers. She was kind and motherly until she found out I was Native. After that she seldom spoke to me, and only came by to collect the rent.

Halfway through the school year the students were asked to take a practicum job placement. I chose the Saskatchewan penitentiary, thinking that I wanted to work with inmates. But two weeks into my practicum, I decided it wasn't for me. The atmosphere was ugly and hard, and I couldn't see myself being a prison guard for the rest of my life.

At some point I lost interest in school, more so the program, and started to think about what I *really* wanted to do. I hadn't given writing much thought — it wasn't a job, nor had I considered it an option. But then I found a school calendar for the

University of Victoria. It had a creative writing program which sounded wonderful, and I sent away for an application. The application arrived a week later, but to my disappointment a sample of my writing was needed. I hadn't written anything in almost a year and the poems I had felt inadequate.

Nevertheless, I made up my mind to get something together. I began writing a stage play — it was the only genre I felt I had any experience with. The play was called *Winter of the Robin* (a dreadful title, now that I think about it); it was about a Métis girl coming home to be with her grandmother, who was dying of cancer. I worked diligently on capturing the idiom of the characters, especially the grandmother, whom I loosely based upon Aunty. My schoolwork slipped behind and it was impossible to catch up. But I didn't care — I had to finish the play!

Finally, a month and a half later, the play was done. Mom sent me the sixty dollars to get it typed up, and when I held the finished manuscript in my hands I felt exhilarated. I sent the application and play off to the university, hoping for the best.

I waited apprehensively until the answer came three weeks later. I had been accepted into the program! I called Mom and told her the good news. In my excitement, I hadn't thought of moving back to B.C. or how I would even get there, let alone how I would pay for tuition. Reality set in and I realized moving to Victoria was impossible. Discouraged as I was, I knew one thing: I had been accepted, which meant I had what it took to be a writer.

I knew by now that I didn't want to stay in school. But I also knew that if I quit, I would lose my living allowance. I half-heartedly tried to catch up on my assignments, but all I wanted to do was write. Finally the co-ordinator of the program called me into her office and very gently told me that I needed to make a decision. There were other people waiting to get into the program and it wasn't fair to take up a seat, especially if I didn't want to be there.

I hesitantly dropped out of school and wondered how I would support myself. I refused to go to welfare. I applied for various jobs, but no one would hire me. Then one afternoon, at the unemployment office, I saw a job posting for what I assumed to be a "writer" at the CBC in Saskatoon. It was too good to be true. I made an appointment to see the woman in charge of hiring. A week later I stood out on the highway and hitched a ride to Saskatoon with the play in my knapsack.

How naive I was! All I could think about was working at the CBC — a prestigious place — as a writer. I was sure the job would be glamorous, and best of all I would finally be doing what I loved the most. I almost have to laugh when I think of that poor, unsuspecting woman who interviewed me. She obviously hadn't expected my enthusiasm, not to mention the look of disappointment that came across my face when I found out the job was for a journalist to broadcast the news. She very kindly explained the job and, before I left, asked to see my play. She said she would read it and jokingly promised to let me know if any "writer" jobs became available.

I found a job as a waiter in a Greek restaurant and moved into a little house across town. The boss was an absolute nightmare to work for and made no attempt to hide his dislike of Native people. Despite my hate for him, I kept my head down and did as I was told. The tips were good and I was able to make a decent home for myself.

By now I had forgotten about the CBC and being a writer. Then one day, out of the clear blue, a producer from CBC Regina called me. He said that he'd read my play and wanted to know if I would be interested in writing a fifteen-minute radio drama. He wanted a traditional but contemporary Native story, and without having the faintest idea of how to write radio drama, I agreed. I had the library order a book from Moose Jaw on how to write radio plays. When it arrived two weeks later, I practically ran home to start work.

I read the book several times, trying to get an idea of the

format, a sense of timing and place. After about three false starts, I put the book away and listened to the story in my head. The characters were all there — the grandmother and her granddaughters, twin sisters, and the handsome Sioux warrior they were both in love with, but I couldn't figure out the structure of the story. I closed my eyes and tried to remember the stories Aunty had told me. Suddenly it became clear. The story would begin from a contemporary time, move into a legend, and then come back to the present.

I scribbled late into the night, as if a voice were telling me what to write down. I felt as if I was actually sitting at the grandmother's table, listening to her story about the two rival twin sisters. I could see her granddaughters sitting there, too, engrossed in the story, setting aside their petty differences to learn something. By the end of the first scene, I already had a title, *The Storyteller.*

In between my shifts at the restaurant, I worked non-stop on the story until it was done. I was pleased with the end result, more so the process of writing it. It was unlike anything I had ever experienced. At times I wanted to give up in frustration, sure that I was a lousy writer. But when I held the finished draft in my hands, I felt as if I'd accomplished something worthwhile.

I sent the story to Regina and a week later received a contract and a cheque for $968.67. It was the most money I had ever received — and it was for my writing! Of course there were rewrites to do, but it didn't matter.

Another voice had somehow broken through the walls of my childhood silence, and it was undeniably mine — a voice that until now had fallen upon my own deaf ears.

Twenty-Two

The Boy of Yesterday

When first I saw rye whisky
get the worst of him
he was smashing everyone in sight.
Hearing my mother scream, I ran downstairs.
My kiddy voice was no match.
She just lay there, convulsing under his
boots.

My mouth still knows what happened:
puffed-up lips I remember.
The rest is hazy, long-ago movie. Someone
yells, "Go to the neighbours, call the cops."
And it ends there

Leaving a disturbed feeling over the years.
Even now, they say, "Greg, forget it."
Going on is made easier because they won't
talk. I talk because I have to.

While I was in school I came across a poster advertising a play about Native land rights in B.C. It starred a young actress named Lauren Peters, and I was positive it was the same person I had gone out with in Vancouver. I hadn't spoken to Lauren in almost two years and had often wondered about her. As the play was being held at the Sturgeon Lake reserve, I made arrangements to go and see it.

The night of the play I sat nervously in the audience, waiting for the lights to go down. Sure enough, the play started and Lauren walked onstage dressed in a button blanket and cedar headband. I felt a lump in my throat: the past had suddenly caught up to me. Yet I was thrilled to see her again, proud that she'd done something with her acting dream.

After the play was over, I stood in the shadows and watched while she conversed with a few admirers. She seemed more beautiful than ever, radiant and self-assured. When I finally screwed up the nerve and went over to talk to her, she threw her arms around me and started to cry. We made arrangements to meet for coffee and I met her a short time later at a Chinese café on Main Street. We talked until dawn and then I walked her back to her hotel. By now she was involved with someone and thinking of marriage. I secretly felt envious, wishing that I had made more of an attempt to stay in touch with her.

The play was running one more night in Prince Albert. Lauren and I got together the next evening and once again talked until dawn. She said that she loved me — had always loved me — and wanted us to be together. I was ecstatic! I imagined us married, settling down and having babies. Ryan had often warned me about getting married too young, but now I didn't care. Lauren was back in my life, and this time I wouldn't be careless enough to let her go.

Such sadness comes over me when I think of that time. I was in such denial of my true self, my sexuality or anything remotely gay. If only someone, back then, had assured me that being gay was as normal as being right- or left-handed — that it wasn't a curse or sickness — I might have understood myself differently. Instead, like so many gay youth, I suffocated my difference, hoping that I would magically be like everyone else. My behaviour makes perfect sense to me now, but that has only come about in the last few years. Learning to accept myself is a continuous process. Embracing my "difference" has been pivotal in my relationship with the Creator, family, and friends. Perhaps even one day, perhaps soon, we will come to respect and embrace each other's differences and find the strength humanity needs in order to carry on.

Lauren and I returned to Vancouver in June 1988. Her sister met us at the airport, and as we were driving into the city I suddenly realized that once again I had left my little house and all of my things behind, abandoned my job, community, and friends. I looked out at the endless freeway, billboards, and buildings and wished I was back on the plane, going home. The smell of the ocean hung heavy in the air. Already I missed the dry Saskatchewan air, the smell of the wheat fields and damp earth after a sudden downpour. I missed my people who had been so much a part of my spiritual growth. I became aware of my own self-defeating actions, and how in the past, I had so recklessly abandoned everything. Why was I always following someone else's life and dreams? Why wasn't I happy enough within myself to pursue my own?

Lauren lived with her boyfriend; she hadn't yet broken up with him. So I stayed with her sister until things could be figured out. But the days turned into weeks and it became evident that she had no intention of asking him to leave. Meanwhile, I was back to no money. My rent in Saskatchewan was due and I was worried about my things. I called my landlord and made up an excuse, promising to send money as soon as I could. Three months went by and I was panic-stricken. I knew I had made a terrible mistake, but there seemed to be no way to fix it. I called some friends in Prince Albert and asked them to pack my things and store them. I seldom saw Lauren any more and I was tired of my own immaturity.

It was back to Maple Ridge, where I stayed with Aunty and Chuck until I could get back on my feet again. By now Aunty had changed so much that I hardly recognized her. She seemed much older, almost as if she'd aged ten years for every one. Her face was no longer bright and animated. Her eyes were dull and lifeless, the mischievousness gone, as if it had disappeared with my childhood. She drank almost non-stop, quarrelling with Chuck over stupid things.

Equally as disturbing was the change in Mom. She looked seventy years old, even though she was only forty-four. And now the signs of lupus were evident. Red, scaly marks covered her face and arms, and her skin was pale and sickly looking. She had lost a lot of weight and her clothes seemed to hang off her small frame. Her eyes were still bright and full of love, only something unrecognizable had come to live there.

Maple Ridge, too, had changed. The apartments and hotels down by the river looked as disreputable as ever; thoroughly neglected yet oddly triumphant, like a ship that had been salvaged from the sea. The people of my childhood had either died or moved away, but it didn't seem to make a difference. Others had taken their place, with the same defeated faces and hollow eyes that I remembered. The children seemed frozen in time, unaware of the ugliness that surrounded them. Their playful shouts rang up and down the street, innocently carrying the promise of tomorrow.

I found a job at a bakery and started to get my life in order. About a month later, unexpectedly, I got a call from another producer from CBC Vancouver. He had gotten my name from the producer in Regina and asked if I would be willing to consult on a radio drama. The story was called "Follow the Buffalo Home" and had been written by a white woman from Winnipeg. It was about a Métis boy and his search for family. Essentially it was a "coming home" story, but it didn't reflect the Native experience accurately. The characters, such as the

Kohkum (grandmother) and *Mosoom* (grandfather) were stoic and one dimensional, speaking as if they'd just learned English. The smattering of Cree throughout the story was obvious and verbose, and I was suspicious of a Cree legend that I'd never heard of.

With the emotional support of my boss, I quit my job and went to work rewriting the entire script. I worked with the actors and taught them Cree, even a song, and I combed the CBC library to find the perfect music score. The drama was produced a month later and I received five hundred dollars for my part. The writer was paid handsomely and flown back to Winnipeg. A short time later, her agent called me and asked me to be "involved" with the script. It was being made into a feature-length movie. When I asked for half of the money and credit, I never heard from her again.

The one good thing about that experience was that I began to understand the role of Native writers: the importance of telling our stories. Just as the history books had been written from a white perspective, so had most of the movies and books about Native people. I searched out books by Native writers and read them with a new sensibility, a new recognition and appreciation. I read such books as Beatrice Culleton's *In Search of April Raintree*, Howard Adams's *Prison of Grass,* and Tomson Highway's *The Rez Sisters.* I re-read Maria Campbell's *Half-Breed.* My first angry response was now replaced with pride and admiration. The book spoke shattering truths and filled me with a different kind of anger — one that was productive.

I began to take a serious interest in poetry. I read various poets, striving to get an idea of the form, a sense of rhythm and movement. I read poems out loud, feeling as if I was singing them, as if that voice in me — the voice of my long-ago dreams — had finally come to life. I sat in cafés until all hours of the morning, scribbling down poems as fast as I could write them. Only now it was different. I mumbled the poems into my hand, having to *hear* them before I wrote them down. I am sure people thought that I was crazy, but I didn't care.

In the fall of 1990, I found a job with the Salvation Army, working with young offenders at a correctional facility. While I was there, I met Trevor, a fourteen-year-old Métis boy who had grown up in foster care. He had been shuffled from one home to the next, and had no connection with his biological family or roots. He was justifiably angry and defiant, and I took it upon myself to adopt him as my "little brother" and help him, just as Ryan had done for me.

I suppose, without fully realizing it at the time, I saw a great deal of myself in Trevor. I identified with his anger and frustration, recognizing my own childhood trauma. I began to realize the tremendous anger I felt towards Mom and my family. The years of abandonment, abuse, alcoholism, and neglect had crippled me emotionally, had shaped my image of the world and myself. And yet somehow my spirit had survived, and with it, the will to carry on, to find some sort of healing and peace.

From somewhere within, the boy of yesterday seemed to be calling me. I knew that I would have to face what had always been there — a child in fear of being abandoned. If the truth of my experience could not change, I could at last learn not to look away.

Twenty-Three

Endings / Beginnings

I kept / praying
for the lush green
of spring / or an end
to the orphaned winter /
until there was nothing
to pray for / hope for /
hold onto / for the last time
I held those same hands
that changed diapers /
gave whippings /
held and spoke volumes /
all in such a short
short time

Shortly after I came back to the coast, I started having terrifying dreams about Mom dying, and I would wake up sobbing. For all our problems, the idea of her dying, of leaving me for good, was inconceivable. I couldn't imagine my life without her.

With Saskatchewan behind me and its hard-earned discoveries, I began to look to my future. I knew there were still many obstacles to overcome, but I finally felt a happiness, a certain hope that the pain of my childhood would find a voice, a way to heal itself. I knew nothing would be able to scar me as it once had.

The greatest gift of coming back to Maple Ridge was healing my relationship with Mom. I suppose in some psychic way, I knew we wouldn't have much longer together, and I wanted to share my discoveries with her. We spent hours looking through old pictures of Grandpa and his family, talking about his past and the pain he must have carried throughout his life. And yet the more we talked, the more I realized a part of him had never renounced the truth. His love of fiddle music, his quiet but strong presence, his gift of generosity and family love, his strength and perseverance had all come from the same spirit of our ancestors.

I strongly believe my trip to Saskatchewan, more so Batoche, was neither coincidental nor unplanned. In many ways, I feel Grandpa had led me there, had wanted me to break the silence of his heritage, to share the gift with my family. Mom immediately embraced being Métis. I recall the pride that came across her face as she thoughtfully fingered one of Grandpa's pictures, nodding her head as if her own childhood questions had suddenly been answered. She then dug out an old program from Batoche Days, July 1967 — a year after I was born, handed it to me, and smiled. She looked at me for a long moment — a moment where everything suddenly makes sense — and said, "Darling, I took you home when you were only a baby."

Over the next few years, my relationship with Mom changed drastically. By now her health was failing and a new, but old, fear settled over me. In my childhood, I had been helpless to control our separation, but now it seemed inevitable and I went out of my way to change it. I felt if I could save her from herself, from the drinking and pills, I could prolong her life, possibly even beat the lupus. But her lifestyle was beyond my control and I was forced to make a decision: either I left her altogether or accepted her as she was.

Although there were many parts I found difficult to accept, I began to realize Mom wasn't just my parent, but an individual, a human being who had known a great deal of pain — someone *I* suddenly realized had the right to make her own choices. Odd as it sounds, I also realized that I really did admire and love her — had always loved her, in spite of her shortcomings. She had always done her best under the circumstances.

I am so grateful for the time we had together, for the opportunity to work through a lot of my childhood issues. Although her death left me with a new pain, a permanent emptiness, her patient ear, loving support, and strong will made a difference in my life and the process of my maturity. How fortunate I have been! The genuine love we shared and expressed, even over a short period, has been more than most children share with their parents over a lifetime.

Besides my involvement with the CBC, I hadn't given writing as a career much thought. The poems I had written were more of a healing exercise, an expression of my feelings, thoughts, and understandings. Many of them were about being Native and concentrated on political and historical themes. In hindsight, I can see they were quite didactic, ranting about the injustices *done* to First Nations people. Other poems were nature-based, typically Native. At the time I didn't give my own life — writing out of my own experience — any credit. Being young and Métis somehow didn't seem to qualify me as a "true Indian writer."

I felt the radio dramas had provided me with a certain amount of experience, had given me a great deal of confidence. Now I wanted to do something different, something inward looking. I dreamed of writing a book, a poetry book.

Once again I searched out books by Native writers, specifically poetry collections and anthologies. Some of the writers spoke to me, although, like my own poetry, I found many of the poems stale, didactic, and poorly written. Nevertheless, I studied them with a critical eye, grappling for my own voice. I knew one thing for certain — I didn't want to write an "Indian" poem for the sake of being Native. I wanted to be a writer, a poet, and speak from a voice that was truly reflective of not only my heritage, but my experience.

In 1992, without any real direction, I began work on *The Gathering: Stones for the Medicine Wheel.* I rewrote most of my original poems, focusing more on a Métis sensibility. The collection seemed to unfold naturally, and I found myself writing more autobiographical pieces. I wanted a spiritual element to the book and looked to the Medicine Wheel as a sort of map. The directions, *North, South, East,* and *West,* became sections in which I was able to chart my spiritual and healing journey.

I sent the manuscript to four different publishers (most of whom, unknown to me at the time, didn't publish poetry) and received rejection letters from all of them. After more rewrites, I sent the manuscript to a publisher in Vancouver. By now I knew getting published was difficult, if not impossible, but I hoped the Grandmothers and Grandfathers were with me just as they'd been with *The Storyteller.*

Two months later, to my surprise, an editor from the house called and said they wanted to publish the book. In my excitement I didn't think to ask about a contract or anything business-like such as advances or publishing details. I gladly agreed to rewrite a lot of the poems, as the editor wanted, and waited for direction. I received the manuscript a few weeks later and was stunned. Every page had comments like "too didactic," "slight," "cryptic," and "polemic." I had no idea what the comments meant or where to go with the book, and in a complete panic, thumbed through the dictionary. I tried my best to redo the poems, but each time I sent them off, they came back more of a mess. This process went on for almost a year until finally I was so frustrated, I blew up. Our publishing "agreement" ended in a heated phone conversation, the editor telling me to "stick to writing short Indian stories" and me yelling "Go fuck yourself!"

Outraged, I sat in the middle of my living-room floor and

shredded the entire manuscript. As I was tearing up the last page, I suddenly flashed back to my time in the hospital. How could I possibly allow myself to be defeated after everything I had gone through? I had something to say and I was bloody well going to say it!

At some point while I was working on the book, I moved in with a girl whom I had known since I was eighteen. Kerry was half Sioux and half Ukrainian, and she came from a very traditional family. She was two years younger and had never lived away from home. We had become good friends over the years, had danced together at powwows, and shared many of the same beliefs. Her father was a spiritual person and had helped Ryan and some of the Peeyaychew boys to Sun Dance and to learn the Sioux ways.

My relationship with Kerry, at the time, was everything I wanted for the future. She was generous and good-natured, kind and traditional. Her face radiated warmth and her brown eyes held the spirit of her grandmothers. She was a skilled beadworker and seamstress and had made outfits for numerous dancers.

I shelved the idea of writing a book and put my energy into work. As much as I enjoyed my job with young offenders, I felt restless and empty. I had come so close to fulfilling my dream, to having my own book of poetry. The months of unprolific silence weighed upon my mind and I half-heartedly started to write again. It seemed as long as I was writing, I was content. The original idea of *The Gathering* had now taken shape and I wrote new poems for the sections. By a complete fluke, I was browsing in a bookstore one day and came across a book of poetry by a mixed-blood writer. The voice of the Native community was so apparent in her work, I decided to approach the publisher. I sent them eight poems and a letter describing my book. I expected nothing, and set myself up for another rejection letter. The phone rang a couple of weeks later. The publisher had read my poems — had liked them — and wanted to send me a contract.

Over the next six months, under the gentle guidance of Julian Ross and Michelle Benjamin of Polestar Book Publishers, I completed *The Gathering*. I wrote close to seventy new poems and included only one in the book from the original collection. The book was in the final stages of production when Julian sent me the galley copy. I stood in the middle of my living room with tears streaming down my face, clutched my dream to my heart and said, "*Kin-na-skomtin Nohkumak ekwa Ni-mosoomak*" (Thank you, Grandmothers and Grandfathers).

I have come to the part of my story which I knew from the beginning would be difficult to write. That December six years ago — ten days before Christmas, to be exact — Mom lay in a coma at St. Paul's Hospital in Vancouver. Death is a very private experience, and I cannot attempt to describe the fear, panic, and anguish of her death. The combination of lupus, drinking, and medication had finally taken its toll. Her legs were paralysed and the doctors discovered cancer of the bowel.

Before her death on January 12, 1993, two very important things occurred. Trevor had come to live with Kerry and me and, although he was in jail most of the time, we managed to give him a sense of family and community. I located his biological family and mother who, in a cruel twist of fate, had been killed in a car accident the previous spring. The ministry, who had placed him in our care, had very little information about his family. In fact, the records they had were incomplete and negative. I refused to give them the information I had, but instead broke the news to Trevor as gently as I could. I didn't want him going through life believing his mother had never loved him or that she'd carelessly given him away. I didn't want him believing the ministry's lies — that his parents were no-good drunken half-breeds.

The other important event was that Mom got to read *The Gathering*. I had taken the galley copy to her while she was hospitalized in Maple Ridge, a month before she was rushed to St. Paul's. She sat up the entire night, reading and re-reading the book. The next day I went to see her was to be one of our last visits.

To this very moment I can see her vividly: sitting there in her hospital bed, her tiny legs now useless, while she held the manuscript in her lap. She reached out and touched my face, marvelling at how grown-up and talented I was. She nodded her head and, in her gentle but assuring way, said, "Greg, I'm so very proud of you. I read your poems last night and couldn't believe *my baby* had written such a wonderful and thoughtful book. You're going to do so much for our community, for the lost ones like Grandpa and me. I know now why God blessed me with you. My son, my blessing, always remember that I love you."

The Gathering came out in April 1993, a few days after Mom's forty-ninth birthday. She had wanted so much to hold the book in her hands. The night of the book launch I looked out at my friends in the audience, at the empty seat I had reserved for her. I felt her presence there, listening to every word that I uttered. I finished my reading and sat down beside Julian, who had tears in his eyes. He shook his head and reached over and patted my shoulder, proud as Mom would have been.

The voice I had searched so long for was now mine. Like Mom, it had been given to me as part of the Creator's great plan for my life. Only now the silence of her passing seemed to bring more voices — voices of my grandfather, Cheechum, and Kohkum Otter — spirit voices that seemed to whisper, "*Osam oke-peko mame-tone-ne-yeh-chee-kunna kakeke-ka-pimatah-see-chick*" (Because only the memories live forever).

Twenty-Four

Thunder Through My Veins

The years following Mom's death have been perhaps the most difficult but fulfilling of my life. I have come to appreciate, though not fully, the enormous strength her death has given me: the innumerable insights into my own character and spirit; the unseen power of the Creator that I have come to rely upon. More and more, her generosity, loyalty, patience, strong will and resolve, her unconditional love reduplicates itself in my own life, and as I grow older I catch glimpses of her, my grandfather, Cheechum and Kohkum Otter in my face — the very blood that runs through my veins.

A year after Mom's death I moved back to Vancouver. By now Trevor had gone to live with his girlfriend's family and Kerry and I had split up. I enrolled in the Native Youth Worker Training Program through the Vancouver Community College, completed the course, and found a job counselling street kids. In many ways, the move back to Vancouver was the beginning of another journey I thought had ended with Kevin. But my mother's death had forced me to re-examine my sexuality once and for all.

It all started after I had gone to see her at St. Paul's. I decided to get my hair cut. I knew that Mom was soon going to die, and keeping to the traditional ways of grieving, I chose to have it cut short. I found a salon on Davie Street, sat numbly in the stylist's chair and looked at myself in the mirror. My hair was fairly long and I was trying to grow it out for braids. I looked so old and tired I hardly recognized the face staring back at me.

"My mother's dying," I vacantly said to the stylist.

He cut my hair, and after he was done I wandered Davie Street aimlessly, thinking back over the years, looking into the faces of strange men. God only knows what I was trying to find, but it felt like something I had missed my entire life. It took me years to realize what I was searching for that day. I was looking for my father, for a man with whom I could feel connected, a man I could embrace and shed twenty-six years' worth of tears for.

I had spent a lifetime looking for that man. In my pain, I was unable to see the truth — accept the abandonment — or deal with it. Instead I became involved in relationships that invariably ended in disappointment and anger. It wasn't until I dealt with the pain and allowed myself to grieve for both parents that I finally understood and began to accept my own sexuality.

My final passage into the gay community was both liberating and disheartening. I was able to identify with other gay people, share a common pride, and celebrate our diversity. Yet all of the things I wanted to escape were still there: the drinking and drugs, the concentration on sex, youth, and beauty, and above all, the seemingly impossible task of ever finding a deep, loving, and committed relationship.

Of course, these things are inherent in both gay and straight communities. But for gay people, especially those living in concentrated gay areas or "ghettos," these elements have become exaggerated and expected by the rest of society, even by some gay people. I now understand how difficult it is for many gay people who maintain a certain structure of beliefs based upon our anti-gay upbringing. A heterosexual model doesn't seem to work. However, in defining "new" rules for ourselves, we sometimes seem to digress further into a world of unhappiness and loneliness. I feel so angry when I think of our empty childhoods; lives that are void of gay images, role models, and healthy relationships; spirits that are forced to bend and conform to society's expectations. I can only hope that in my lifetime I will be afforded the same rights and privileges most heterosexual people take for granted. I hope one day to fall in love, have a child, and raise it with my partner.

I did a great deal of writing after Mom died, mostly in journals and in the form of short erotic stories that had nothing to do with being Native, but being gay. I am almost embarrassed by these stories now, although I realize they were simply a reflection of my need for emotional escape. But in all fairness, I must give them credit for helping me to express my desires, poetic sensibilities, and ultimately the fusion of two voices that would reflect my spirit distinctly.

I couldn't seem to find the motivation to write another book, let alone any poems that connected me spiritually to the Creator or my people. I felt that being gay had somehow destroyed my place in the Native community. I feared my writing would be seen as less credible if I "came out," and I would bring shame upon myself and those who had mentored me. Also, very few people knew about my past and I wanted to keep it that way.

Then, in 1994, I received word that *The Gathering* had been short-listed for a B.C. Book Award. I attended the ceremony with my best friend, Kelli Spiers, and my publisher, Michelle Benjamin. At last the Dorothy Livesay Poetry Prize was announced and *The Gathering* was chosen as the best book of poetry for 1994. Shocked, I practically soared up to the stage and stood there with people like Pierre Berton and Margaret Atwood. I was so nervous, I barely recall what I said. However, I do remember acknowledging Mom and the Métis community.

The following day the *Vancouver Sun* announced the winners and noted that I had given the "most memorable speech."

After *The Gathering* came out, I received invitations to give readings at various academic institutions and writing festivals. I wasn't prepared for public life and found it extremely difficult. My shy nature made it almost impossible to give a good reading. I hated speaking in public and couldn't keep from shaking (a trait that I discovered I shared with my favourite writer, Margaret Laurence). I was also asked to do various media interviews and, instead of being selective, I practically spilled out my entire life, only to be upset upon reading the interviews. It took a great deal of thought and practice, but over time I lost my fear of public speaking. I was more thoughtful in interviews and began to select certain topics beforehand, my motivation coming from a certain article that read, "Scofield grew up in a family of drunken half-breeds . . . ."

My work with street kids was not the ideal job I thought it would be. Soon the novelty wore off and I felt deeply affected by the appalling conditions they lived under. Virtually all of them had escaped abusive homes and ended up in Vancouver, on Granville Street, panhandling and using heroin or other drugs. Most of them slept on the street or took refuge in old abandoned buildings, living in squats until the police evicted them. Many, if not all, of the young women were lured into prostitution, falling victim to pimps who promised them love and security. As well, many of the young men became involved with "sugar daddies" who, in exchange for sex, gave them clothes, money, food, drugs, or a place to sleep.

Although my job was primarily focused on street youth, I also worked with adults, most of whom were involved with the sex trade. I learned a great deal about the politics of the street and the dehumanizing effect it had upon the people trapped there. The women who worked "high track" were under the complete control of their pimps who determined everything from their hair colour and style to where they lived and with whom they associated. The transgendered prostitutes worked independently, without pimps, and were subject to a great deal of violence. Many of them were Native and had come from remote communities across Canada. Some had been on the street since they were twelve and were intravenous drug users and HIV-positive. The men in Boystown also worked independently, and in addition to the high rate of violence and drug use, many were also HIV-positive.

The conditions on the downtown eastside were even worse. East Hastings Street overflowed with young Native people, many of whom had grown up in foster care. The IV drug use, prostitution, and violence was extreme, as was the alarming rate of HIV infection. "Shooting galleries" (abandoned buildings and hotel rooms used to shoot heroin) and flophouses seemed to thrive on every block, and people wandered the street vacant-eyed and "tweaking" with uncontrollable body spasms.

Youth organizations such as Street Youth Services and the Downtown Eastside Youth Activities Society worked night and day to provide clean needles, condoms, food, shelter, and counselling. Workers such as myself tried our best to help, but it was futile. The kids, even the adults, were so damaged that it was virtually impossible to get them off the street. Although there were a few success stories, more ended in suicide, overdose, murder, or AIDS-related illnesses.

At some point I became fairly desensitized to the shocking realities of street life. I recall, at first, feeling grateful for being spared the misery of the streets — a reality that could have easily been mine. But over time I came to realize that I wouldn't be able to stay in this type of work for very long. I had the understanding, empathy, and desire to help, but I didn't have the fortitude to carry on. The demands of the clients, more so the unspoken band-aid policies of the organizations seemed only to entrench problems more. The lack of Native workers and the understanding of issues in relation to Native youth was startling and troublesome. I found myself becoming more and more upset at the ever-rising statistics of suicide, murder, and overdose. I believed that giving out condoms and clean needles, like helping people to get on welfare, was a temporary solution to a long-term problem. And yet I didn't know what the answer was. However, I did know that I wanted to voice these issues and try to make some sort of difference.

With this in mind, I began writing poems about street life and all of the things that filled me with despair and rage. I sat in grimy cafés on Hastings Street, striving to capture glimpses of skid row, primarily the lives of Native people: our struggles, stories, and strength. Many of the poems had a general theme, dealing with stereotypes and the oppressive attitudes Native people have encountered for years.

As in *The Gathering*, I found myself writing autobiographical poems, wanting to parallel my own experiences with those of other Native people — mostly the youth. I also wrote poems about being gay. The issues and struggles of gay Native people, at least those on the street, were just as important and relevant to my poetry. I suppose subconsciously I hoped to challenge the Native community, to bring about an awareness, perhaps even an understanding of the hate and homophobia within our own circles. All too often I had heard stories about people dying of AIDS whose families and communities had disowned them, leaving them to die alone in the city.

In the spring of 1996, *Native Canadiana: Songs from the Urban Rez* was published. Once again Polestar Book Publishers, notably Michelle Benjamin, agreed to publish the book and arranged for me to work with the remarkable poet Patrick Lane. I hadn't worked with an editor before, except Julian Ross, who had edited *The Gathering* and had since left Polestar. Needless to say, the idea of working closely with an editor, namely a white poet, caused me a great deal of doubt, not to mention a subtle but not-so-silent hostility.

I first met Patrick and his partner, the acclaimed poet Lorna Crozier, in the fall of 1995. They were in Vancouver doing various readings and promotional engagements. Patrick and I had breakfast one morning to discuss the book, and much to my surprise, I immediately liked him. He was deeply kind and intuitive, genuine and straightforward. Nothing I had written seemed to faze him or make him uncomfortable, not even the gay poems. Instead, he discussed my poems as if they were masterpieces. He talked at great length about his own childhood and young adulthood, the importance of good writing and keeping true to the voice behind the poems. That day he instilled such a great confidence in me, I felt as if I could *truly* write a good book.

Some of the poems, as Patrick bluntly put it, were "lounge acts" and needed to be pulled from the collection. Initially I was hurt and angry, but I soon realized he was right. I needed to get to the meat and bones behind the poems, and so over the next six months I worked continually until the book was done. Many times I called to read him poems and he would exclaim, "You got it, kid!" Looking back, I'm so grateful that the Creator brought our paths together. Over the years, Patrick's support, advice, and encouragement have made a profound difference in my life and work. The day we met, I knew in my heart that if ever I had the choice to pick a father, it would have been him.

Equally as important has been my friendship and business relationship with Michelle Benjamin. Her belief in me and my work has essentially given me the confidence and courage to write. Her gift of quiet patience, sound advice, loving support, and desire to nurture and promote those seldom-heard voices in Canadian poetry and literature is a godsend — a gift that any young, starry-eyed writer would be grateful to receive. In many ways, my relationship with Michelle has transcended the usual author-publisher relationship. I think of her very much as family, a soulmate with whom I've been able to share the greatest pain and, fortunately, the greatest accolades.

After *Native Canadiana* came out, I found myself busy with readings and speaking engagements across the country. I certainly hadn't expected the enormous response to the book, nor had I expected the Native community to support it. Life on the road was difficult, not to mention the great amount of energy it took to be in front of people. The glitz and glamour of being a writer started to fade, and I began to realize the limitations of being a "young, angry, gay Métis poet."

Secretly I felt resentful that my work, and the perception of it, restricted me to such labels. I felt angry at my lack of privacy and the limitations my writing seemed to impose. I felt as if I were living under a microscope, as if everyone was examining *the poor Métis boy who had turned his horrible life into a success story.* Always, the labels. I had struggled so hard to make my dream come true — to find a voice with which to speak – and now all I wanted to do was crawl under my bed and stay there. I realize now that between travelling and my job, it was virtually impossible to maintain a steady flow of energy. Some days I felt so tired I couldn't imagine writing another book. Finally the demands of my writing life became so great that I left my job. Luckily, I was able to get by on writing grants from places like the B.C. Arts Council and the Canada Council. (As Canadian writers, we are extremely fortunate to have these organizations, which enable us to devote our time and energies to writing.)

On the heels of *Native Canadiana,* I began work on a new project: a collection of love poems that seemed to come from a spiritual place. The poems seemed to spill out on to the page, and as I wrote, I felt as if I were in a trance, as if I was taking part in a sacred ceremony. My every dream and desire in relation to love came to life, and for the first time I connected to the unspeakable longing I carried within.

I finally felt like a *real* poet. I hadn't received any kind of formal training and I hadn't the slightest idea of technique or form. My previous poems had come from a more unpolished place, and I thought of them more like stories. But now I was conscious of form and technique, and I strove to create poems that were highly lyrical: songs that were rich with the images of the northern landscape and Cree language. I called Michelle practically every day and read her poems over the phone, wanting desperately to share my new and heightened sense of the world. The more I explored my own desires, the freer I felt. I was overcome by the power of words, the power of language and imagery. Many of the poems came to me in Cree, and in keeping true to *their* spirit and rhythm, I wrote them this way. Furthermore, my most significant experiences of love — love between men — seemed to find a natural voice.

peyis ekwa e-tipskak ekwa
oh, ekwa ka-kemowak,
ka-kemowak

earth smells, love medicine
seeping into my bones
and I knew
his wind voice
catching
the sleeping leaves.

oh, ekwa ka-kemowak,
ka-kemowak

I dreamed
him weaving spider threads
into my hair,
fingers of firefly
buzzing ears, the song

his flute
stealing clouds from my eyes

ka-kemowak
I woke

numb in my bones.

peyis ekwa e-tipskak ekwa
oh, ka-kemowak
ka-kemowak
At last it was night
oh, how it rained,
it rained.

Love Medicine and One Song was published by Polestar in the spring of 1997. For me, the book was very much, and still is, the "baby" of my work to date. Through it and the process of writing it, I was finally able to break down the walls of my own internalized homophobia, set free at last the voice of my own spirit — give back my gift to God, as Mom once told me.

A short time after *Love Medicine* was published, I moved back to Maple Ridge. Aunty Georgina had died the previous spring under questionable circumstances. The police alluded to foul play, but nothing ever came of it. They maintained that she was drunk and had fallen. Chuck and various other people were questioned, but by the time the stories were gathered, they were so confusing the file was closed. Her death, like Mom's, left me with an inexplicable emptiness, only it was different — harder in some ways — as there were questions surrounding her death. I still carry an overwhelming sense of anger towards the police, even society, for so thoughtlessly overlooking the death of yet an another Native woman, dismissing one of the most important people in my life as just another drunken Indian — another statistic.

Aunty was buried in Maple Ridge, thousands of miles from the jack pine, birch, and spruce trees, the wild roses of her childhood. Often, I go to her grave — to the graves of Mom and Grandpa, and sit there, silently talking to them as if the years mean nothing, as if their departure from this world is only an illusion. My fear of abandonment is gone, and in its place lives the memory of two women whose love and support shaped my life. Inside, I keep their stories alive, as I do them. They are in my veins, flowing through my blood. The circle of life goes on.

When I first began this memoir, I thought a great deal about Maria Campbell — about *Half-Breed* — how she had first come into my life, and how over the years she has become my friend, sister, and mother. I have purposefully left out this part of my life, as I have done with others, because I wish to keep it private. I share this now in the context of my own story — wanting to stress the significance Maria's book had for my life and essentially my career as a writer. Perhaps one day another young Métis writer will read my book and become angry enough to write his or her own story.

The process of writing this book has been unlike anything I've ever experienced before. I didn't anticipate the enormous amount of strength it would take to complete it. Many times, I felt like abandoning the whole idea. At times, the pain of the past was so intense I had to virtually force myself to get out of bed in the morning. Some days, I did nothing but cry, yell at unsuspecting people, swear, lift weights, or go for long walks.

My walks always led me to the same place: back to that part of town where I had spent so many hours, dreaming of an escape. I suppose, without fully realizing it, I was looking for the boy of my childhood, who I knew had the words to tell the story. But the more I looked for him, the harder it was to write.

At some point, I learned to be patient and became reconciled to waiting. I allowed my mind to skip over the murky water of the Fraser River, to float aimlessly on the log booms. I allowed my eyes to simply wander the streets and buildings of that long-ago time, unobtrusively and without pain. And I allowed my heart to be weightless, almost as if I was a stranger passing through this part of town.

More and more, the boy began to show himself. I would catch glimpses of him: poking around in the bush for treasures, sitting on the dock by the river, picking candies at the Chinese corner store, playing in old abandoned cars and the dumpster behind the funeral chapel, knocking upon Aunty's door or the door of the bootlegger, looking for his mother.

Then one day, by complete surprise, I found myself sitting on the steps outside the apartment, my tears falling silently to the ground. Somewhere in the distance I could hear my mother's cries, her pleading, and the sound of my stepfather's fearful voice. I put my arms around myself and rocked back and forth until I could feel the strength of my own fatherly arms. I closed my eyes and found my mother in bed, holding her swollen face, offering up a hopeful smile. Behind her smile sat my stepfather, his dark eyes moving like poisonous snakes. Holding the boy, I stood before him and sang the snakes to blindness. He neither flinched nor cried out, but grew smaller and smaller until he became a pile of words.

I gathered the words, the picture of the Iron Soldier, the boy, and his mother and put them in the basket of my heart. The hotels and apartments, the houses and shacks, the numerous towns and faces seemed to settle into the past and fade into a colourless memory, taking with them the unspeakable pain of my childhood.

Only the river remained timeless and enduring. Its dark murky surface suddenly became clear like a mirror, reflecting back my grown face: the rocks, twigs, leaves, and bones of my journey.

The boy I had searched for was safe at last. Finally, I was free to grieve, to laugh, and to dream.

Dark clouds began to gather in the west and a light rain danced upon the river. Walking home, I remembered the dream I had once had about Kohkum Otter.

"*Noosim*" (Grandson), she had said, grinding charcoal and spit, painting a thin black line down the middle of my face, "this is your path of life, the path of two worlds in which you walk.

"*Sawonohk*" (South), she continued, mixing pollen and spit, covering the right side of my face, "the time of innocence and maturity. These gifts you will always possess.

"*Pan-ke-see-mowtuk*" (West), she continued, marking four black dots on my left cheek, "the time of the spirits and the Thunderers. Listen closely, for they will give you songs and stories. You will go through four phases in your life. And when you have completed your path, you will come to your ancestors."

"*Noosim*," she added, "my blood flows through your veins. The Thunderers have touched you.

"*Haw*," she clapped, "*ne-kumow*! *ne-kumow*!" Now, sing! Sing!

Acknowledgements

The process of writing this memoir has been much like walking through a dark forest, coming upon unexpected visitors whom I hadn't made room for. In many cases, I was just as surprised to find the pages filling up with their presence. Of course, I had made provisions for such characters as my mother, Aunty, Grandmother(s), stepfather, Kevin, Yvette, Ryan, Alana, and a few of my writing mentors and publishing associates. The others have merely worked their way out of my subconscious, finding their place in the story.

My best friend, Kelli Speirs, whom I've known for twelve years, and whom I love immeasurably, commented that the book was only reflective of my Native/gay experience; that because she was white and heterosexual there was no place for her in my story. Although I was initially perturbed, I knew to a large degree that she was right. If I were to write about her — characterize her — it would only be in the sense that our friendship crossed those invisible lines of age, race, and sexuality. Because the book concentrated on my search for belonging, I would have completely whitewashed the essence of our friendship. The history of pain, love, triumph and family ties we share means a great deal more to me. But still, I was torn as to whether I should write about her as my *first white friend* or not write about her at all. I mulled it over, as I did with so many other important people in my life, and in the end decided to keep her private. It has nothing to do with age, race, or sexuality. Simply, these people are my *family*, my support system, my greatest confidants.

Some people I have deliberately omitted from the story because the pain of those relationships is recent and still part of my healing. Perhaps one day I will write about them. Perhaps even they, too, will resurface. Until then, I carry them inside, as they slowly work their way to my heart — the place where all stories are born.

This book has been a long-standing dream, and I am grateful to the many people who have supported me. It would be impossible to list them all, or to even do them justice. I would however like to acknowledge my editor, Phyllis Bruce, whose encouragement, insight, and constant support have brought this book to life. Also, my love and gratitude to Michelle Benjamin, Kelli Speirs, Maria Campbell, Patrick Lane, and Lorna Crozier for believing in me every step of the way. Thanks to the Writers' Development Trust and the Canada Council for their most generous financial support.

I have learned a great deal about myself and the process by which I have become an adult. As I mentioned in the Foreword, I am neither the victim or oppressor. If anything, I am a survivor — and the world is full of survivors. I am neither unique nor different. My story, in one way or another, has been told hundreds of times and will be told again and again. As long as our stories continue, so will the healing. The circle of life will continue.

Poems Quoted

from *The Gathering: Stones for the Medicine Wheel*

pg. vii/ "Between Sides"

pg. 1/ "Thinking of Father on This Day"

pg. 51/ "Saint Mother"

pg. 105/ "The Spirits Have Begun Working"

pg. 131/ "Deceiving Honour"

pg. 174/ "Talking Because I Have To"

from *Native Canadiana: Songs from the Urban Rez*

pg. 6/ "Blood Secret" from "Three Poems (legacy in the blood)"

pg. 12/ "1966" from "*ni-acimon*/Autobiography"

pg. 32/ "Treats"

pg. 36/ "The Poet Takes It upon Himself to Speak" (excerpt)

pg. 48/ "Stepfather"

pg. 93/ "Kiddy Psych Ward" (excerpt)

pg. 154/ "1985" (excerpt) from "*ni-acimon*/Autobiography"

pp. 158 & 167/ "1986" (excerpt) from "*ni-acimon*/Autobiography"

pg. 180/ "*ochichisa*/her hands" (excerpt)

from *Love Medicine and One Song*

pg. 195/ "His Flute, My Ears"